IMAGES
of Modern America

KINGS DOMINION

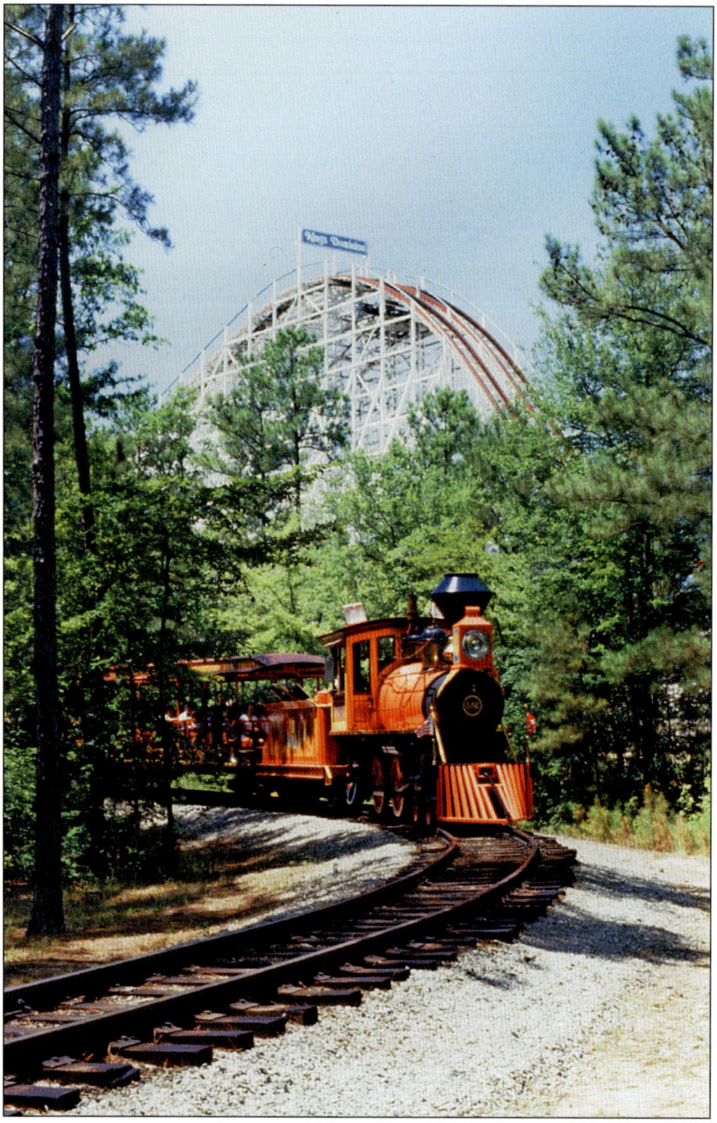

Kings Dominion's first full season in 1975 featured a number of rides and attractions. The Old Dominion Line was a 36-gauge railroad with two steam trains that gave guests a relaxing ride through the forests of Old Virginia. In the background is Rebel Yell, a large wooden racing roller coaster that reigned as the king of the park's thrill rides. (Courtesy Kings Dominion.)

On the Front Cover: Clockwise from top left:
Intimidator 305 (Author's collection; see page 86), Lion Country Safari (Courtesy Kings Dominion; see page 22), Old Dominion Line (Courtesy Kings Dominion; see page 18), Hanna-Barbera Water Follies (Courtesy Kings Dominion; see page 56), King Kobra (Courtesy Kings Dominion; see page 44)

On the Back Cover: Clockwise from top left:
Sky Ride (Courtesy Kings Dominion; see page 28), Apple Turnover (Courtesy Kings Dominion; see page 40), Eiffel Tower (Author's collection; see page 14)

IMAGES
of Modern America

KINGS DOMINION

Scott N. Rutherford
Foreword by Dennis Speigel

ARCADIA
PUBLISHING

ISBN 978-1-4671-2301-3

Published by Arcadia Publishing
Charleston, South Carolina

Printed in the United States of America

Library of Congress Control Number: 2014947955

For all general information, please contact Arcadia Publishing:
Telephone 843-853-2070
Fax 843-853-0044
E-mail sales@arcadiapublishing.com
For customer service and orders:
Toll-Free 1-888-313-2665

Visit us on the Internet at www.arcadiapublishing.com

For Brian K. Plemmons, my constant companion in roller coasters, amusement parks, and various other adventures. Thank you for being there.

Contents

Foreword

I was the general manager of Kings Dominion when it opened, and at age 29, I was the youngest person to hold that title in the industry. Kings Dominion's $60 million capital investment was second only to Walt Disney World at the time.

I am proud to say that the park was built on budget and on time (actually two weeks ahead of schedule). Opening day was history making in our industry. On May 3, 1975, at 7:00 a.m., traffic backed up 10 miles north and south on I-95 and on the two state routes servicing the park. The park was scheduled to open at 10:00 a.m., but by 9:00 a.m. we had already admitted 50,000 raucous, excited guests. To stave off a potentially serious situation that we knew was going to be less than desirable, we closed the gates—making Kings Dominion the only theme park ever to close before it was officially opened to the public.

In the nine years I led the park, we opened amazing rides (the first encapsulated-themed ride complex in the industry, the Lost World, was definitely ahead of its time); defeated a major teamster organizing attempt; and I began a regrettably short-lived acting career in the motion picture *Rollercoaster*, filmed on location at Kings Dominion by Universal Studios and starring George Segal, Richard Widmark, and Henry Fonda, giants in the film industry. Helen Hunt also made her debut appearance in this film with somewhat greater subsequent success. This was the first time a major motion picture had ever been filmed in a nationally acclaimed theme park. Kings Dominion helped balance out the historical tourism for which Virginia was known by providing fun family entertainment to the state's five million plus annual tourists.

Kings Dominion brought to Hanover County—basically a rural sleepy neighbor to the city of Richmond—a thriving economic boom filled with new recognition, thousands of jobs, major tax base increases, and a level of excitement never before seen in the agricultural-based county.

Kings Dominion was, and remains, a wonderful place to work and visit. Scott's book captures the park's history with flair and accuracy.

—Dennis Speigel

ACKNOWLEDGMENTS

It would be quite impossible to include every Kings Dominion ride, attraction, show, or restaurant that ever operated in a single volume. Instead, the purpose of this book is to offer a number of candid snapshots in time—both historical and contemporary—in an attempt to show a portion of the highlights that have made this unique theme park so very exceptional over the past 40 years.

I would like to thank a number of individuals who assisted me along the way. Their contribution in bringing this book to life was invaluable and are listed as follows: Dennis Speigel, Kings Dominion's John Taylor, Greg Talley, and Katelyn Curry, Phyllis Rutherford, Brian Plemmons, Michael Boodley, B. Derek Shaw, Gary Slade, Terry Lind, Jeffrey Siefert, Tim Baldwin, Richard Munch, Tony Rice and the KD Golden Years team, Frank and Teresa Purtiman, Roy Brashears, and, of course, my editor, Gillian Nicol, and all the good folks at Arcadia.

Unless otherwise noted, all images in this book come from Kings Dominion's archives.

INTRODUCTION

Kings Dominion was built during a prolific period of growth in the fledgling American theme park industry. From 1961 to 1975, an unparalleled number of parks opened across the United States. Following in the footsteps of Six Flags Over Texas, which debuted in 1961, this parks utilized the pay-one-price (POP) method of admission, which allowed guests to enjoy virtually everything aside from food and merchandise for the price of a single ticket.

Kings Dominion was built as direct result of the success of Kings Island, a theme park that had opened in Mason, Ohio, in 1972. Owned by Family Leisure Centers (a partnership comprised of the Taft Broadcasting Company and Top Value Enterprises), Kings Island was the successor of Coney Island, a beloved traditional park that operated near Cincinnati (1886–1971). Based on Kings Island's popularity, FLC decided to expand with a second property. Focusing efforts on the mid-Atlantic region, FLC purchased 1,500 acres of farmland at $2,500 per acre. The site in Doswell, Virginia, was chosen due its proximity to the population centers of Richmond, Norfolk, and Washington, DC.

Construction began on October 1, 1972. The general layout of the park would resemble that of Kings Island, in that a central corridor (International Street) lined with shops and restaurants would feature fountains leading to an Eiffel Tower, with themed "lands" radiating outward.

To generate interest in the project, a Preview Center opened to visitors in 1974. Highlighted by Lion Country Safari, a live animal African-themed drive-through attraction, the Preview Center also featured the Scooby-Doo wooden roller coaster and various exhibits that gave visitors an idea of the wonders they would find when Kings Dominion fully opened the following spring.

Sporting a price tag of $60 million, Kings Dominion was at that time second only to Walt Disney World as the most expensive theme park ever built. The remainder of the park officially debuted on May 3, 1975. Turnout on opening day was nothing short of overwhelming. More than 50,000 visitors poured through the front gates that morning, while an estimated 60,000 were turned away when the park reached its maximum capacity before 9:00 a.m. Attendance for the park's inaugural season was an impressive 1.5 million. This was especially significant with another Virginia theme park—Busch Gardens: The Old Country—opening the same year 60 miles away.

Along with Lion Country Safari and its new monorail replacing the automobile drive-through aspect, Kings Dominion's first season featured International Street and four other themed sections: Coney Island, Happy Land of Hanna-Barbera, Old Virginia, and Lion Country Safari. In addition to the Eiffel Tower, the park was home to a total of 15 rides, as well as a number of games, live shows, dining options, and other attractions.

Over the next several years, the park continued to grow. The sophomore season saw the introduction of an Enterprise (Apple Turnover), Flying Bobs (Matterhorn), Bayern Curve (Mount Kilimanjaro), and Calypso. In 1977, Kings Dominion was one of the amusement parks utilized as a film set for Universal's *Rollercoaster*. A coaster-riding marathon on Rebel Yell held to promote the movie resulted in the formation of the American Coaster Enthusiasts (ACE), an international organization dedicated to the enjoyment and preservation of roller coasters worldwide. That same season saw the addition of King Kobra, one of the world's first steel shuttle loop roller coasters.

The Kings Dominion Campground came online in 1978, while the following year brought the opening of Lost World Mountain that featured three rides built in and around the mountain facade (Voyage to Atlantis, Time Shaft, and Journey to the Land of Dooz). Between 1980 and 1981, the themed area inside the park became known as Safari Village while the monorail that traveled out to Lion Country Safari would be known as the Wild Animal Safari Monorail. The next seasons would see more major attractions added, including the Grizzly wooden coaster (1982) and White Water Canyon rapids ride (1983).

Taft Broadcasting Company sold its theme park division in late 1983 for $167 million to Kings Entertainment Company (KECO). One of the first additions under the new company was an Intamin AG looping starship ride (Berserker) in 1984. In 1986, a TOGO stand-up roller coaster (Shockwave) was added. A waterslide complex (Racing Rivers) opened in 1987, while North America's only Mack Bobsled coaster (Avalanche) followed in 1988. Anaconda, a multi-looping steel coaster, arrived in 1991.

In 1993, KECO's involvement with Kings Dominion ended when the park became one of five North American properties that comprised Paramount Parks. The name was officially changed to Paramount's Kings Dominion, and so began a time of explosive growth as well as the removal and re-branding of several rides, attractions, and areas of the park. During the Paramount years (1993–2006), a substantial amount of capital was utilized and a wide assortment of rides were themed to Paramount films and television shows, transforming the park from something unique to a place that was exceedingly "Hollywood." Removed at the close of the 1993 season, Lion County Safari was one of the first victims of what many refer to as the "Paramount Purge." While new features were indeed added, such as the Wayne's World area and its Hurler wooden coaster (1994) and Nickelodeon Splat City (1995), just as many beloved favorites were summarily discarded, including the Old Dominion Line, Haunted River, Time Shaft, and the Sky Ride.

Though Paramount did infuse the park with a significant amount of cash that allowed amazing rides such as Volcano: The Blast Coaster, Drop Zone: Stunt Tower, Italian Job Stunt Coaster, and Outer Limits: Flight of Fear to be built, they also took away much of what made the original park so wonderful. Other fatalities of the so-called purge include Diamond Falls and the partial removal of the Hanna-Barbera brand.

Early in the 2006 season, it was clear that Paramount was on its way out of the picture. The rumors were confirmed on June 30, 2006, when Cedar Fair purchased Paramount Parks. For many, this was seen as a much needed breath of fresh air with the park beginning a return to its roots. Immediately, the name reverted back to Kings Dominion, while anything associated with Paramount was systematically stripped away.

From then through the present, Cedar Fair invested heavily in Kings Dominion, providing the park with an impressive roster of rides and attractions, such as Intimidator 305, Snoopy's Starlight Spectacular, WindSeeker, Dinosaurs Alive!, the world's largest *Peanuts*-themed children's area, and a major expansion of WaterWorks for the 2015 season.

Kings Dominion's 40th Celebration was launched in 2014 to mark four decades of family fun in Virginia. Returning fun favorites included the reintroduction of the Candy Apple Grove midway, the Clown Band, and the Singing Mushrooms. With the 40th Celebration continuing into 2015, Kings Dominion's future is secure as one of North America's most popular regional theme parks.

One

Preview and Construction

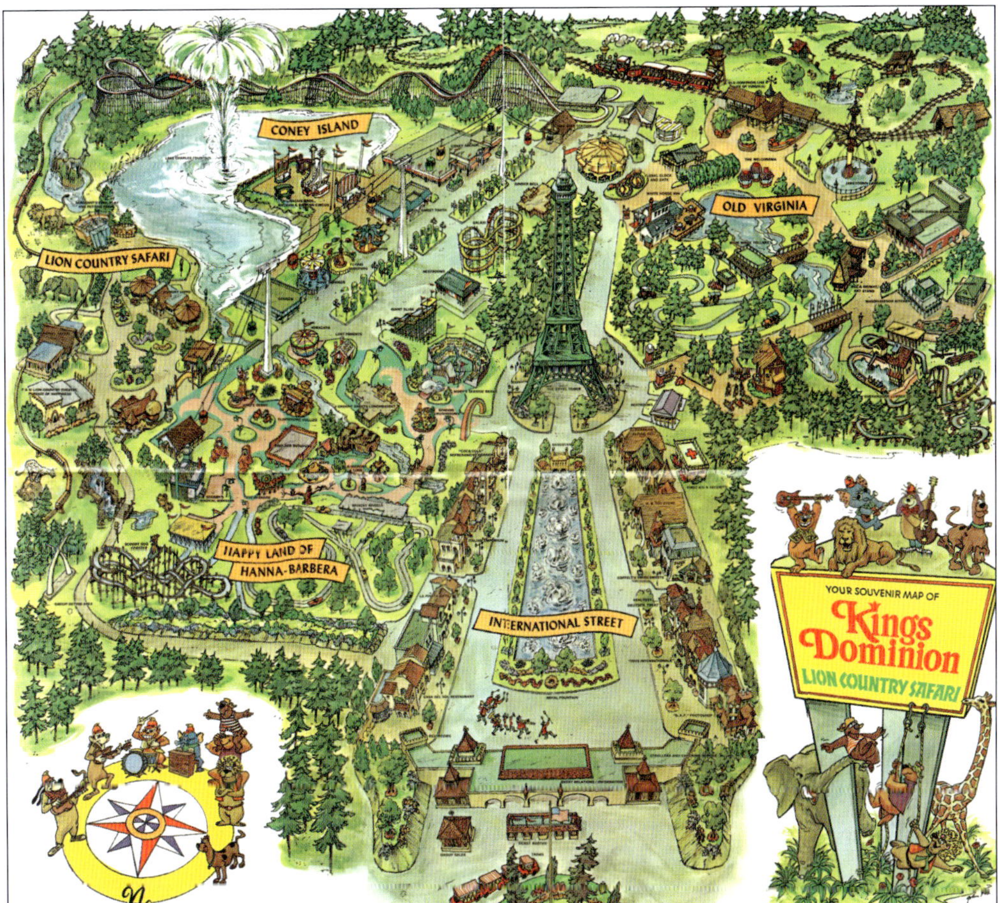

This colorful park map illustrates all that Kings Dominion would have to offer when it opened for its inaugural season in 1975. The park's five themed areas included Coney Island, Happy Land of Hanna-Barbera, Old Virginia, and Lion Country Safari. The presence of the Hanna-Barbera characters is clearly evident. Also represented on the map is Lion Country Safari, a drive-through attraction that opened in 1974 as part of the Preview Center.

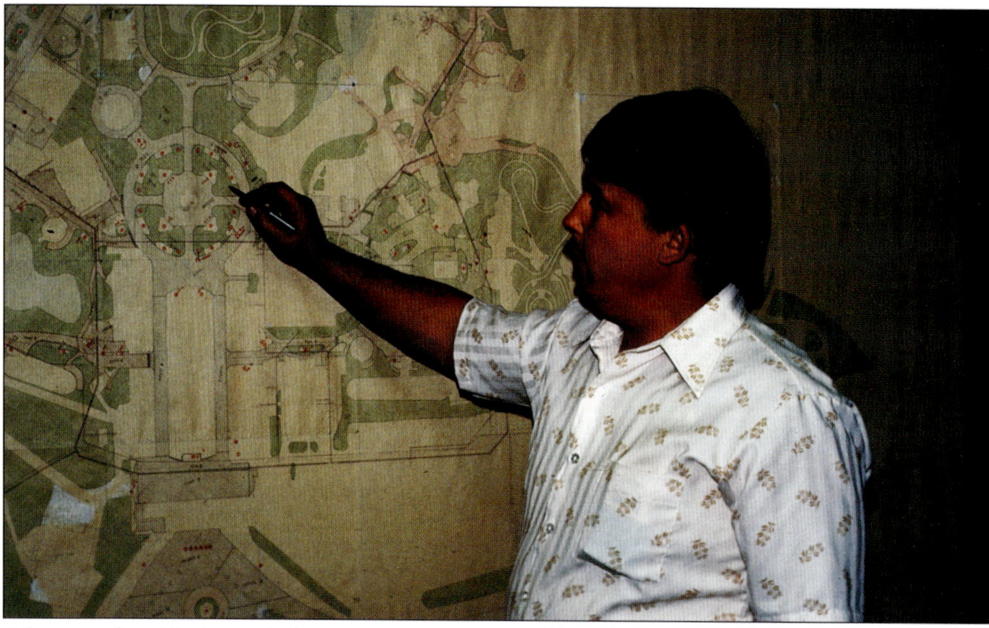

After months of design and planning, construction on Kings Dominion officially began on October 1, 1972. Carrying a price tag of $60 million, it would be the second most expensive theme park project in North America's history. Only Florida's Walt Disney World, which opened in 1971, would surpass it.

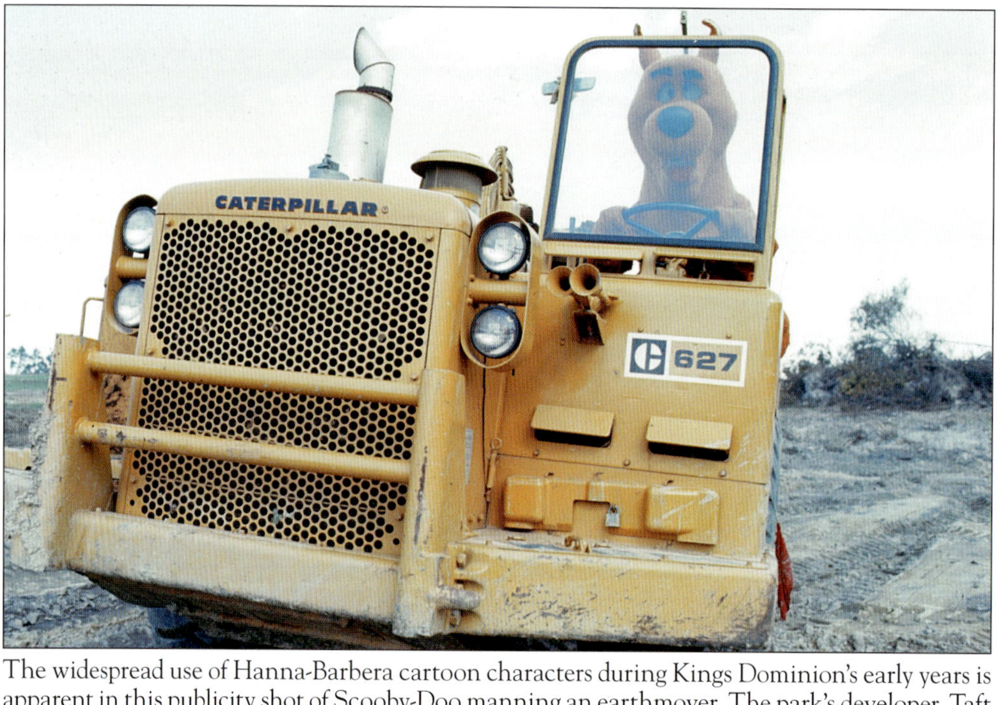

The widespread use of Hanna-Barbera cartoon characters during Kings Dominion's early years is apparent in this publicity shot of Scooby-Doo manning an earthmover. The park's developer, Taft Broadcasting, had purchased the Hanna-Barbera cartoon studio from its founders in 1967. The Hanna-Barbera characters were widely utilized at sister park Kings Island and later at Carowinds, near Charlotte, North Carolina.

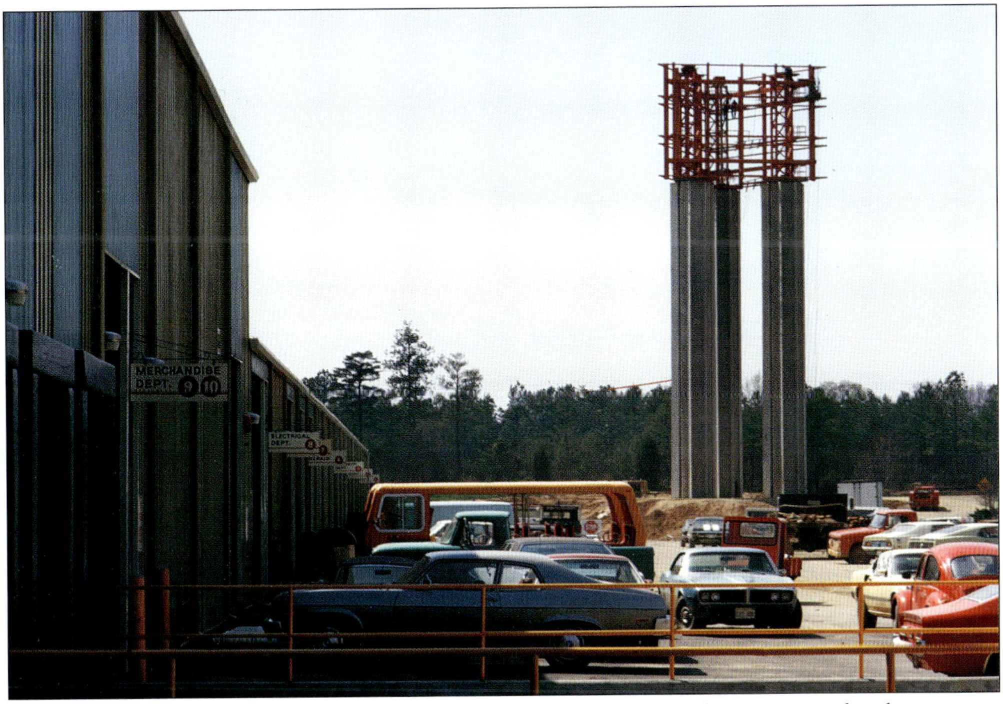

This early backstage view shows the three sturdy columns providing support for the massive triangular marquis that will eventually feature the Kings Dominion logo (along with that of Lion Country Safari) as it takes shape at the edge of the park's property bordering Interstate 95.

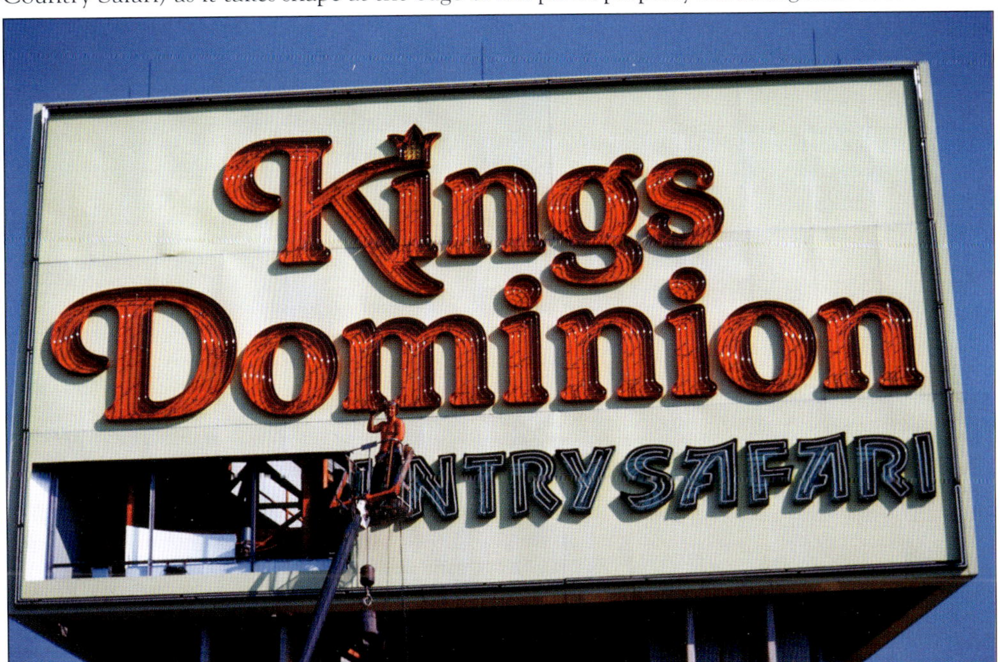

A worker puts the finishing touches on the park's signature sign. Officials worked closely with the State of Virginia to establish and construct north and southbound exits off the interstate to serve Kings Dominion.

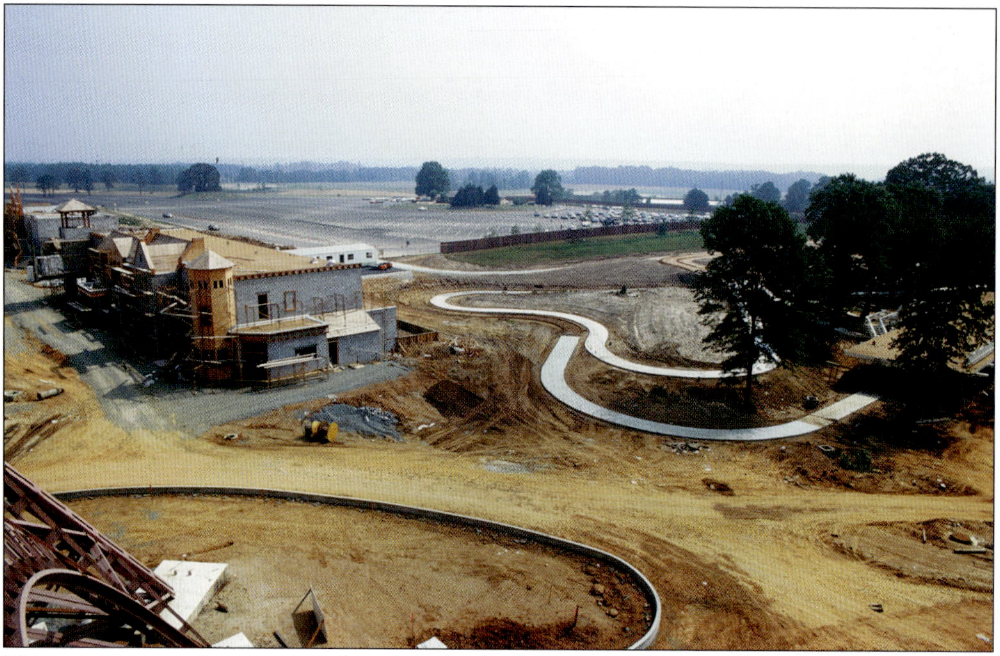

This construction shot captures the east side of International Street. Visible at bottom left is one leg and arch of the Eiffel Tower, which was unpainted and still being assembled at the time of this photograph. The winding concrete path at right will serve as the "highway" for the Wacky Wheels auto ride in the Happy Land of Hanna-Barbera.

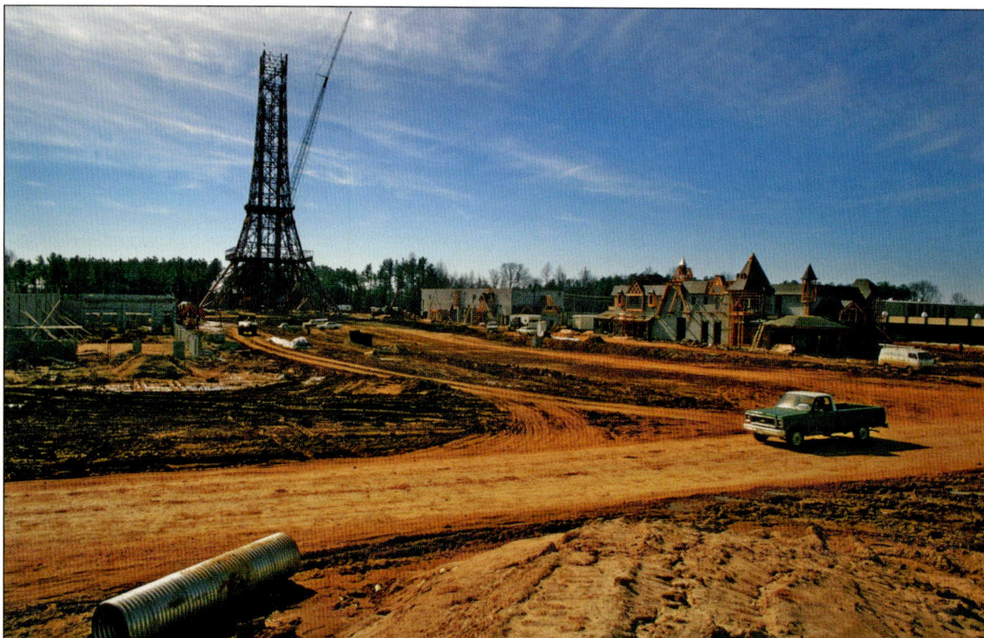

Supplied by Swiss ride broker and manufacturer Intamin AG, Kings Dominion's Eiffel Tower is a one-third-scale replica of the original that opened in Paris, France, during the 1889 world's fair. Once complete, the Eiffel Tower stood 315 feet tall. An identical tower opened at King Island in 1972.

High-flying construction workers brave a chilling winter wind and temperatures near freezing as they labor to assemble the Eiffel Tower. The section pictured will eventually serve as the lower level of the two-floor observation platform at the 265-foot-high level atop the tower.

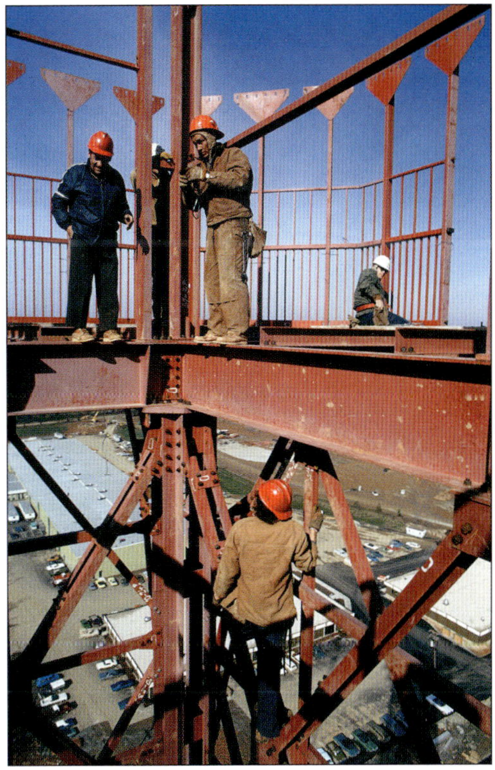

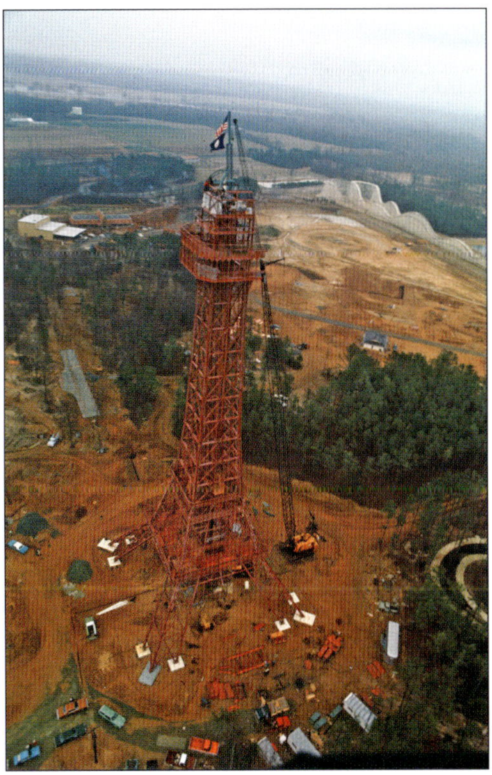

A large crane is used to enact the time-honored custom of topping out. The placing of both American and Virginia state flags signifies that the crew has reached the highest portion of the Eiffel Tower construction project. The Rebel Yell is visible in the photograph's upper right corner.

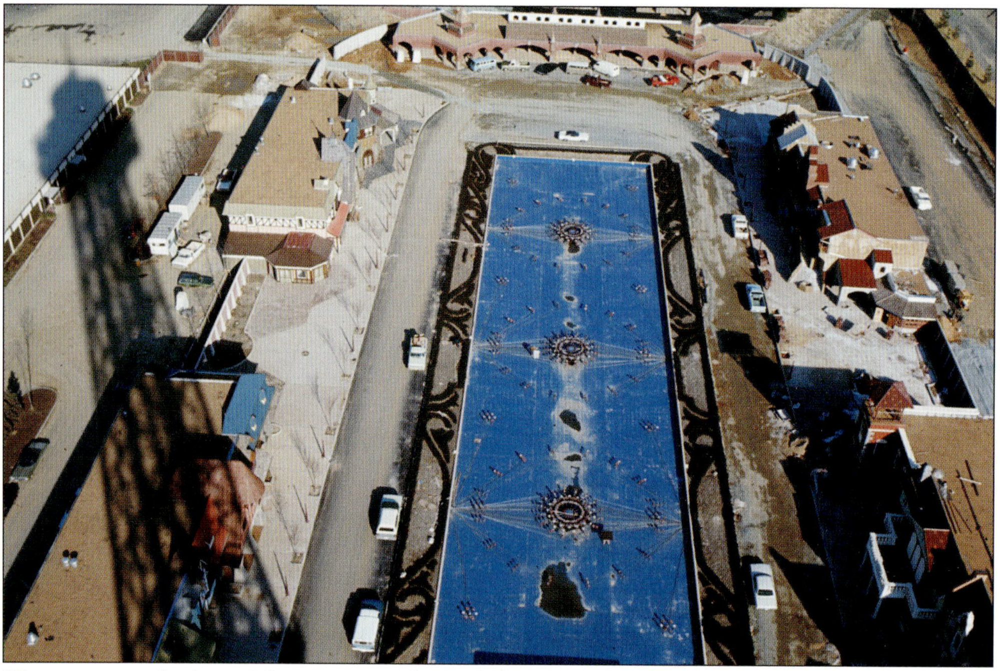

The imposing shadow of the now-complete Eiffel Tower looms large over International Street as construction continues. Concrete work on the Royal Fountain is finished. The ticketing center and main entrance are located at the top of this image.

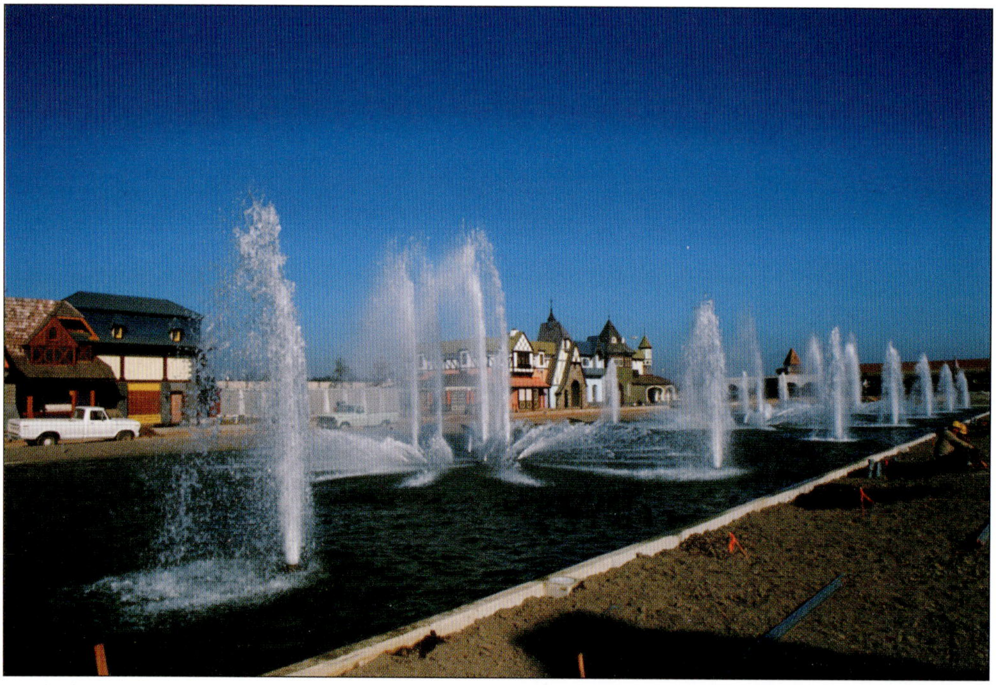

With the remaining work on the International Street buildings being mainly cosmetic, the Royal Fountain is fully filled and tested for the first time. In addition to the fountain's water works, it will also feature an impressive after-dark show thanks to an extensive submerged lighting package.

Holding the smaller model on which it was based, Hub Acton (head of the Kings Dominion fiberglass department) stands before the replica Liberty Bell that is under construction. Once completed, this iconic symbol of American independence will be placed in the park's Old Virginia area.

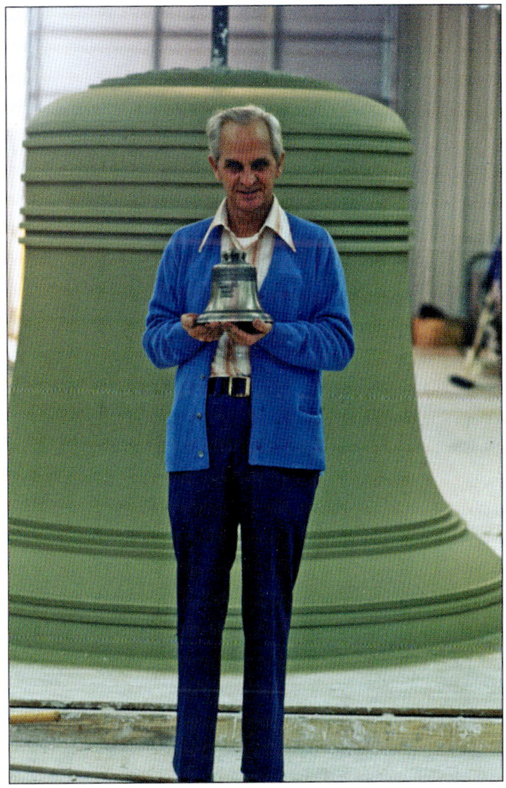

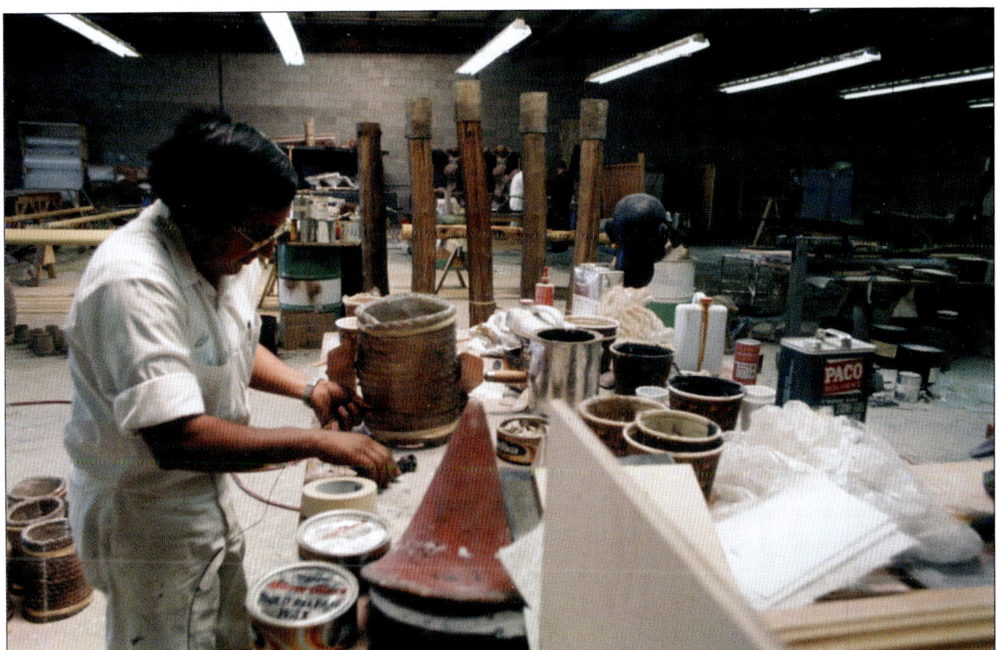

Kings Dominion's shops were busy places during the multiyear construction phase. Here, a craftsman prepares a finial for one of the rustic props that will soon be placed in Lion Country Safari. Many of the park's one-of-a-kind decorations were designed and fabricated on-site in Virginia.

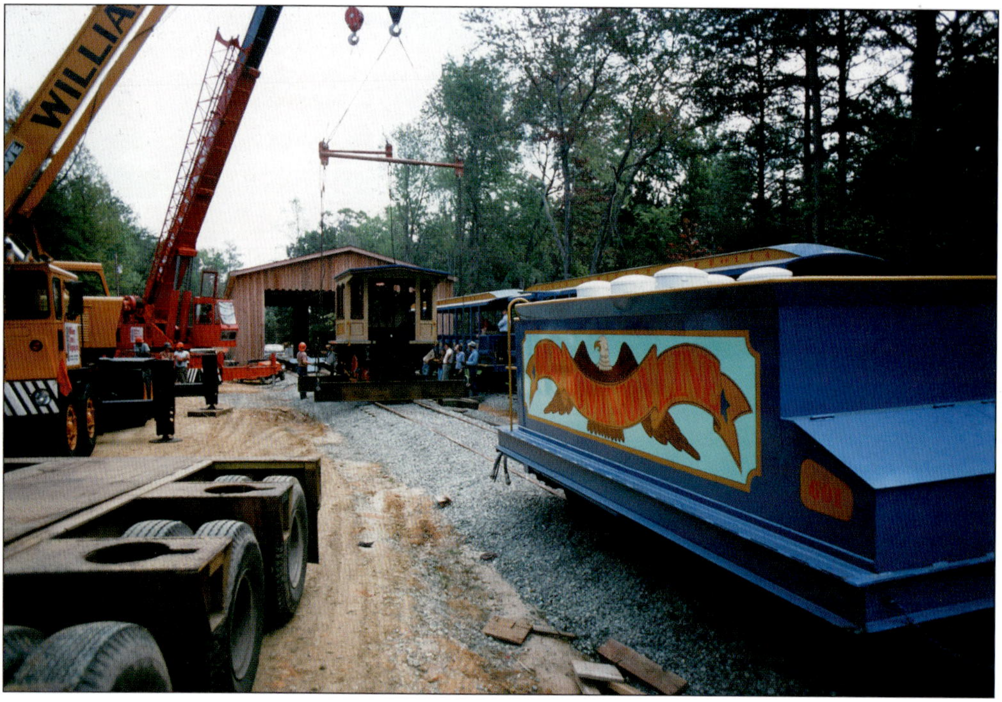

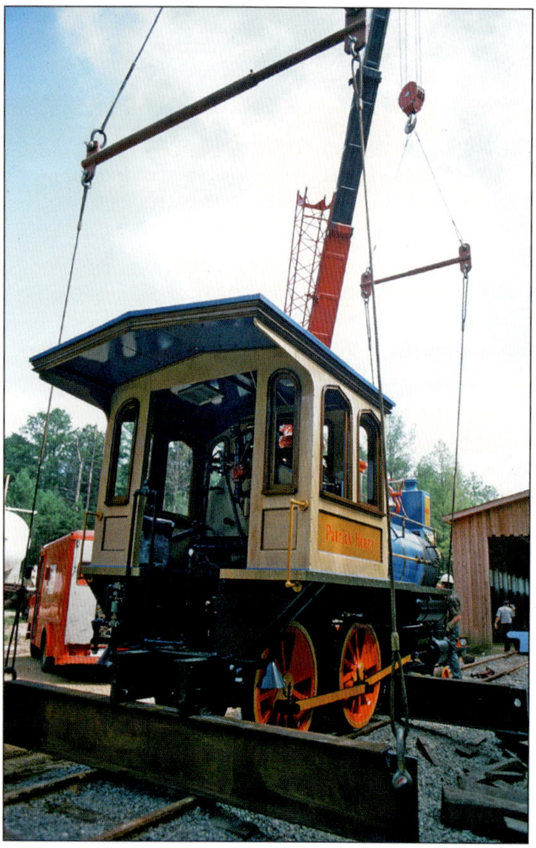

The Old Dominion Line steam train was one of the Kings Dominion's first attractions. Supplied by Crown Metal Products of Pennsylvania, the two trains were comprised of their locomotives and were accompanied by tenders and several open-air passenger coaches (partially visible on a spur at far right).

Here, a crane lowers one of the heavy engines onto the main track of the park's Old Dominion Line. The railroad's two locomotives—the *Stonewall Jackson* and the *Patrick Henry*—were each named after historically important Virginians.

Kings Dominion's Old Dominion Line was no toy train. It was a real, full-sized railroad that required competent operators. Here, an engineer is at the controls of a locomotive during the commissioning procedure prior to the park's opening.

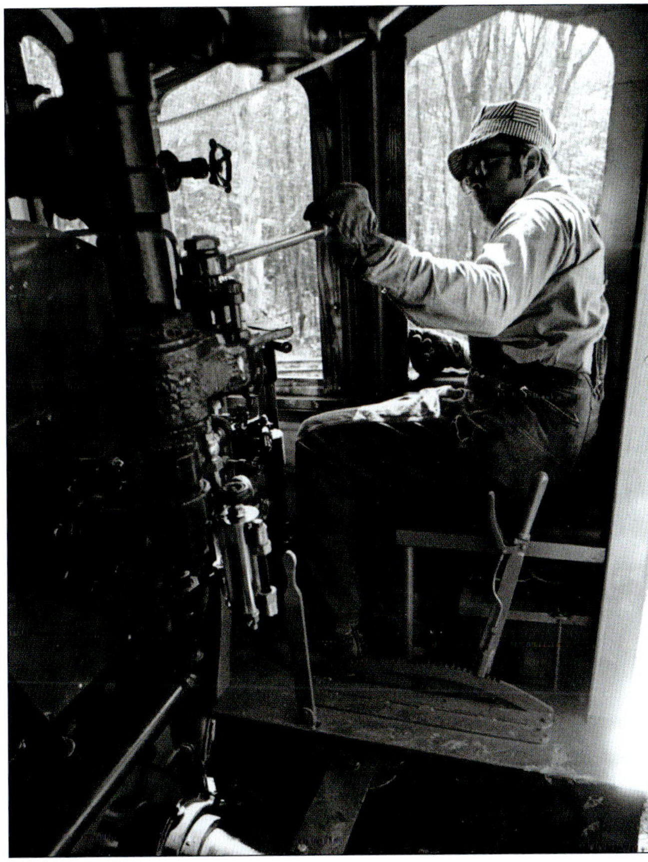

Steam billows from the stack of the *Patrick Henry*—seen here pulling its tender and a single passenger coach—as it inches away from the depot on a test run. During normal operation, each train would consist of multiple coaches. Riders aboard the Old Dominion Line were treated to a leisurely trip through the forests of Old Virginia and the town of Tumble Gulch.

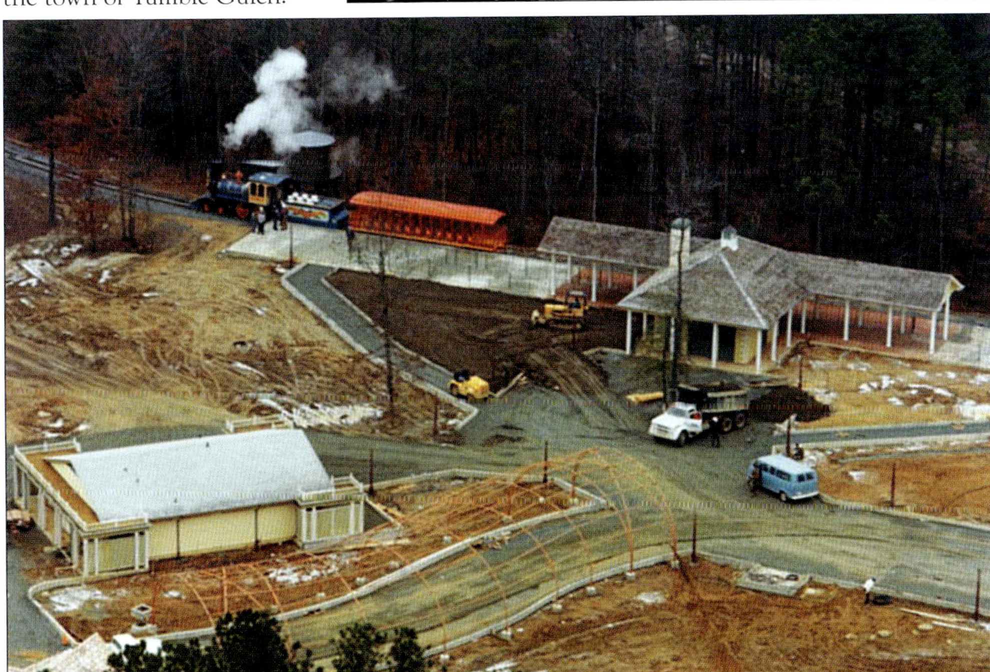

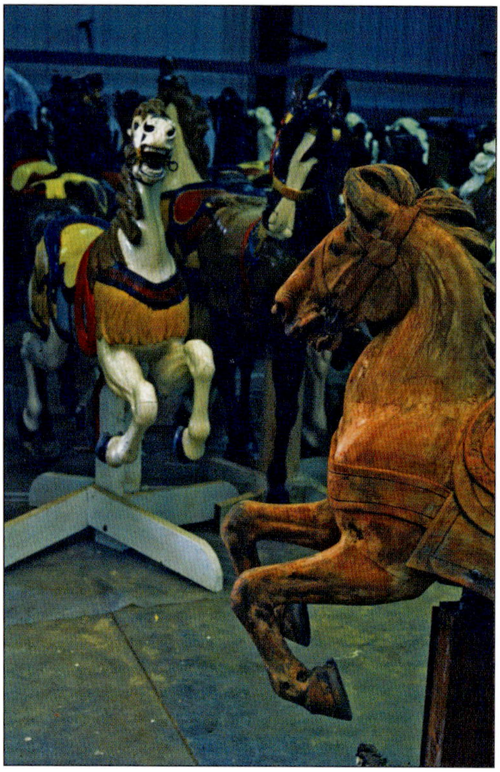

Kings Dominion's magnificent hand-carved wooden carousel has led a long and colorful life. Built in 1917 by the Philadelphia Toboggan Company (PTC), the carousel started entertaining riders at Riverside Park in Springfield, Massachusetts (1917–1938), before being relocated to Roger Williams Park in Providence, Rhode Island (1938–1973). It has operated continuously in Virginia from 1975 to the present.

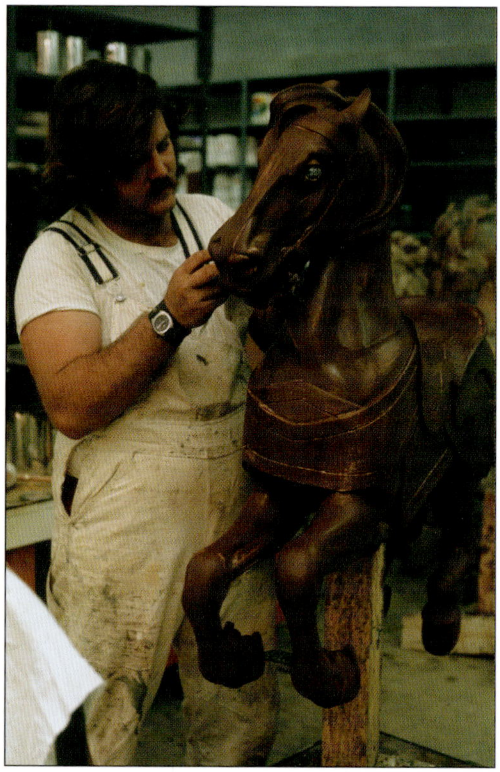

Before being placed into service at Kings Dominion, park officials commissioned a full restoration of PTC carousel No. 44. The many layers of paint (up to 50 on some horses) were removed all the way down to the original wood. Any horses or other parts of the carousel that needed structural repair were given special attention.

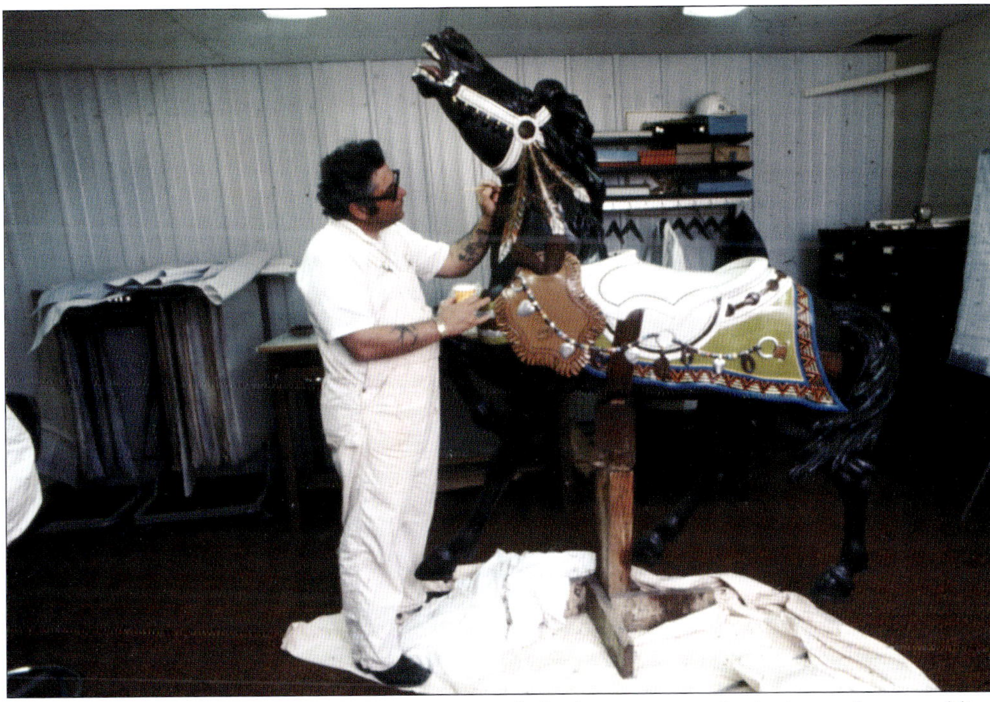

Once all the horses and other figures were repaired, the long process of painting and reassembling began. Here, a craftsman uses a small brush to paint the delicate feathers attached to the bridle of this proud steed. Often, more than 20 separate colors would be required.

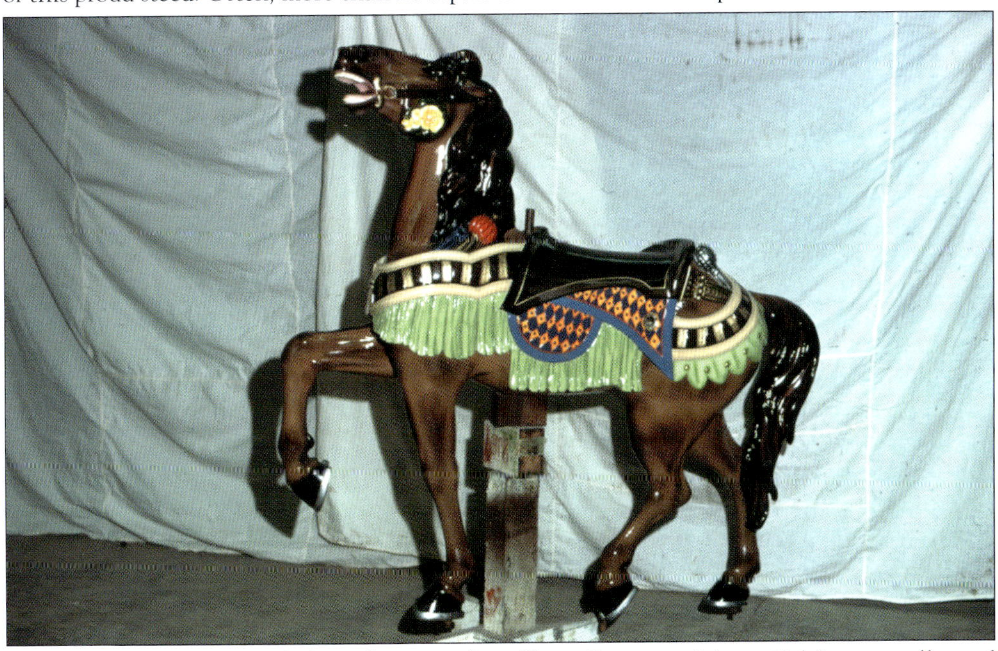

This stunning horse is fresh from the paint shop. Kings Dominion's beautiful four-row, all-wood carousel features 50 jumping horses, 16 standing horses, and 2 ornate chariots on a 56-foot-diameter platform. The machine is housed within an Art Nouveau pavilion topped with a cupola that features trumpeting figures.

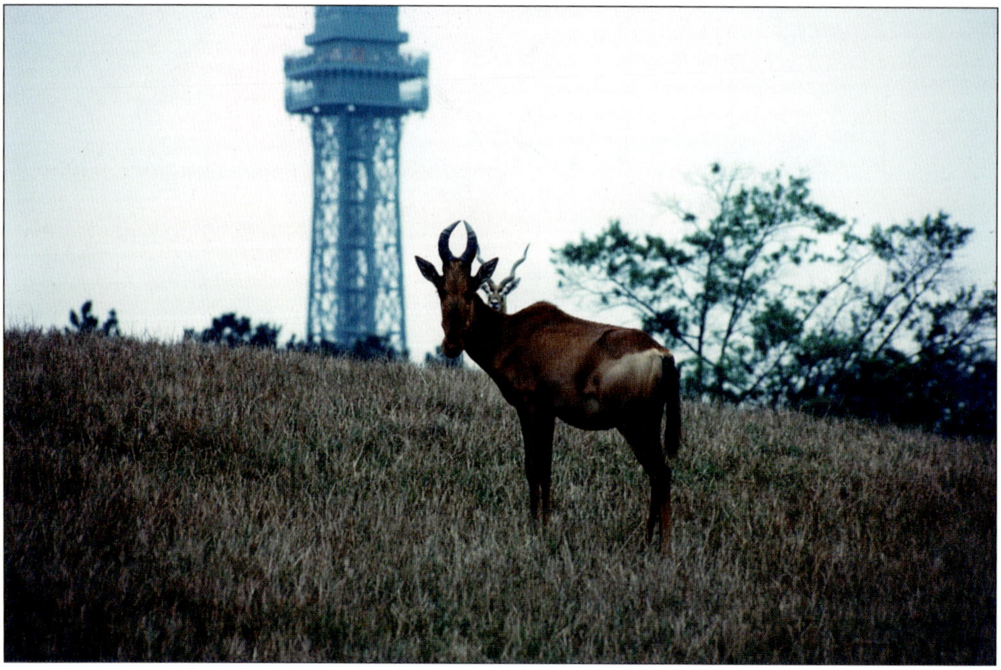

Lion Country Safari, a wild animal preserve, opened in 1974 as part of the Preview Center for Kings Dominion. In its first year, the three-mile automobile drive-through preserve included over 100 different types of birds and animals as well as a petting zoo for families to enjoy.

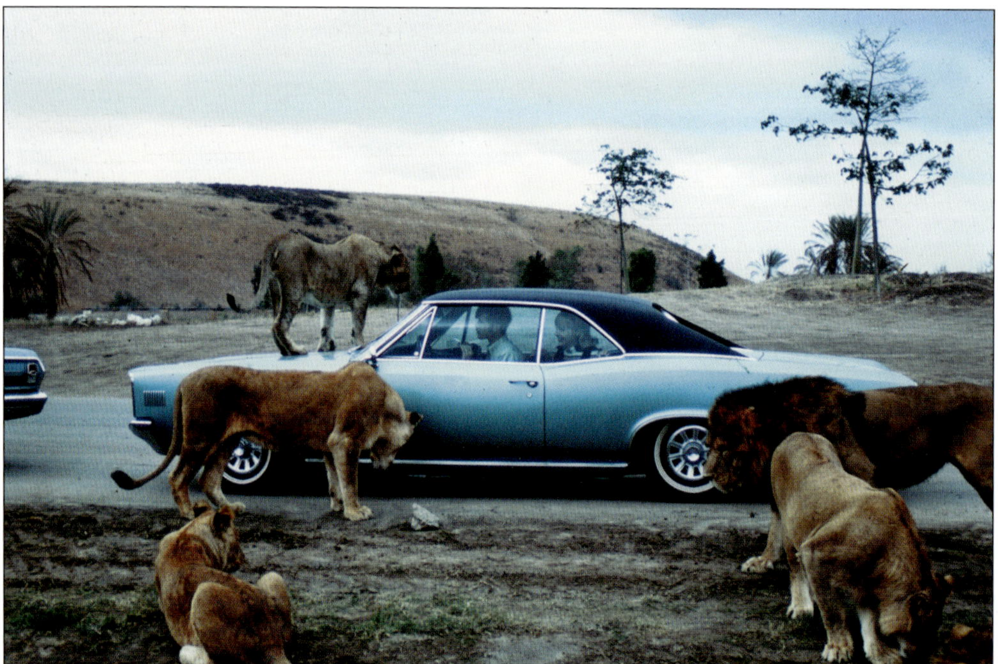

The signature lions of Lion Country Safari became so accustomed to automobiles that they would often climb atop them when drivers slowed or stopped. The park replaced a lot of guest's tires that first season since the lions had a tendency to bite into and shred them.

Park officials quickly discovered that operating a live animal attraction was far different and more demanding than a regular theme park. They hired a team of handlers and caregivers to maintain control of the facility. This lion cub was one of many animals born at Kings Dominion.

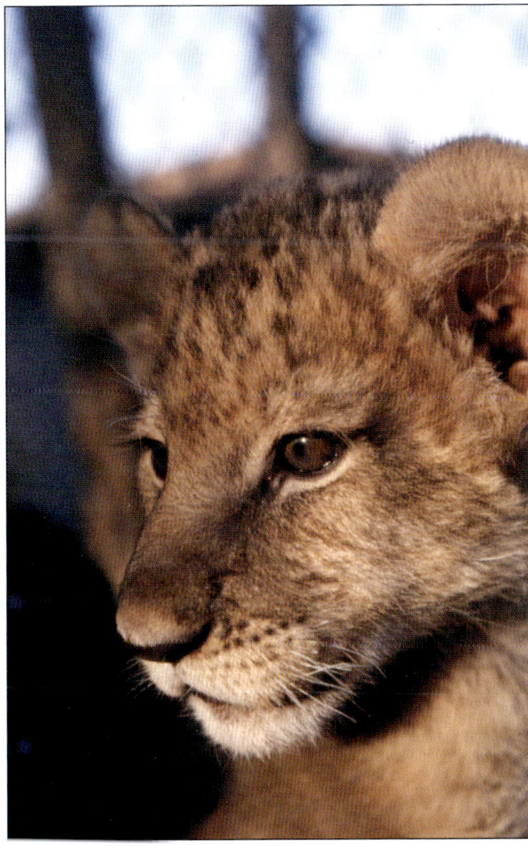

Both adult and juvenile zebras were just a fraction of the creatures guests would encounter during a visit to Lion Country Safari. At the time, four other LCS attractions were in operation in addition to Kings Dominion's version. They included those in Ohio (at sister park Kings Island), California, Florida, and Texas.

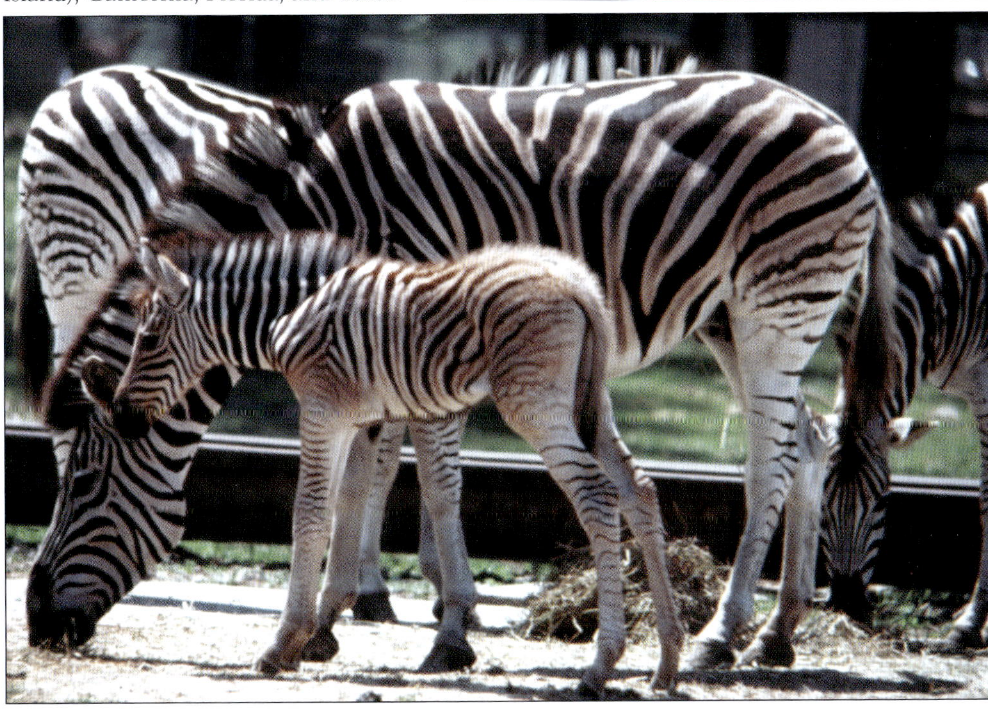

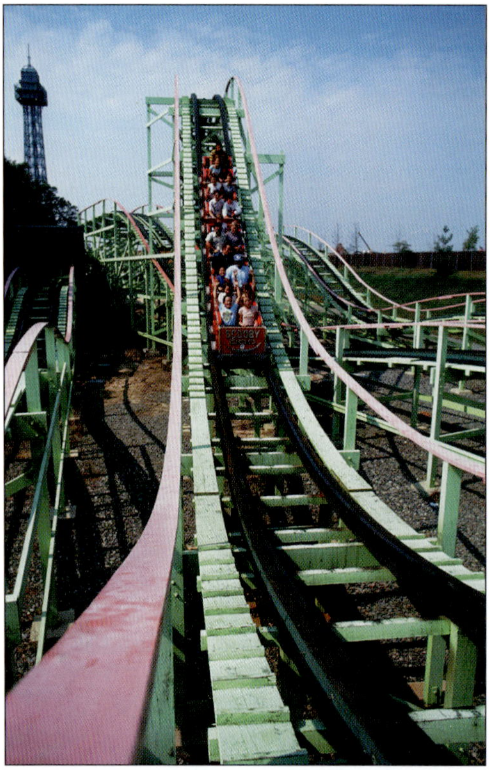

The Preview Center also featured the Scooby-Doo junior wooden roller coaster. A product of the Philadelphia Toboggan Company, Scooby-Doo was a design that would be utilized at other parks, including Kings Island, Carowinds, Canada's Wonderland, and Wonderland Sydney in Australia. The Preview Center's final 1974 attendance figure of 672,000 far exceeded what had been projected.

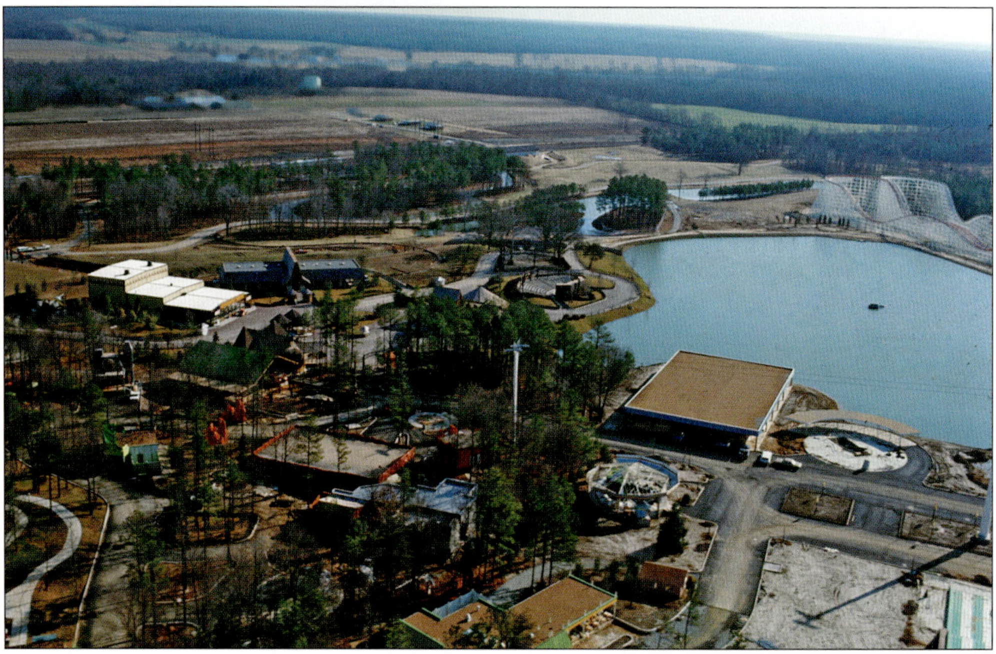

This early 1975 aerial shot captures the park during the very final phases of construction. The station and monorail for Lion Country Safari (top of photograph) and the Rebel Yell wooden racing coaster (far right) are now complete. Lake Charles has been filled in, and the focus now seems to be on the Coney Island midway (lower right).

Two

Grand Opening

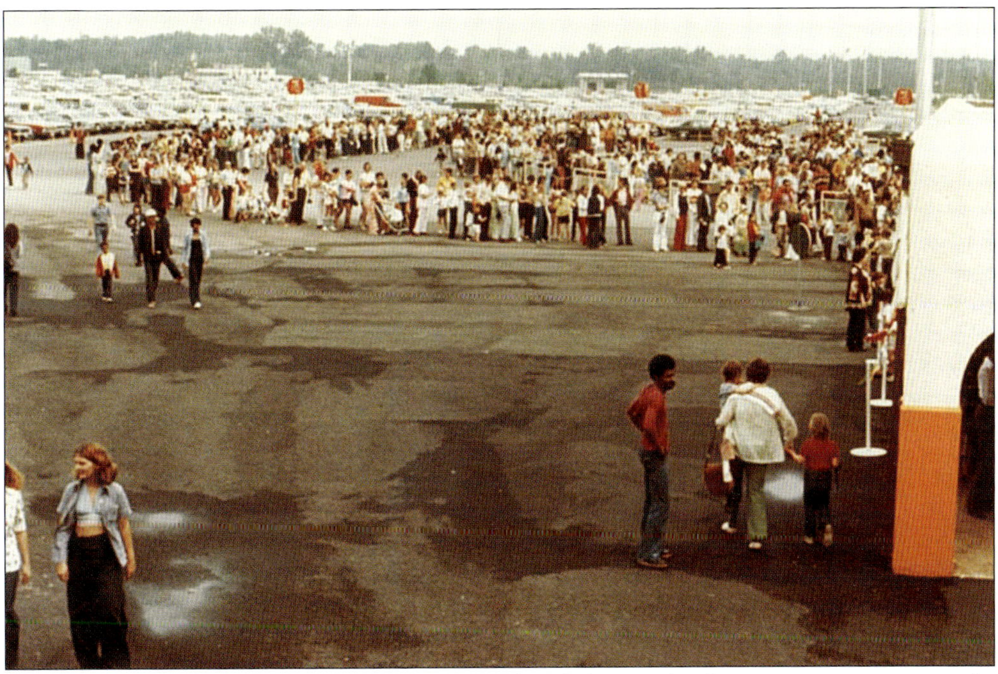

Kings Dominion's opening day—May 3, 1975—found thousands of guests arriving quite early. Traffic congestion backed up for miles up and down I-95 as well as each of the secondary routes leading to the park. This view at the front gate that morning shows a fraction of the 50,000 visitors waiting for a chance to enter. More than 60,000 others were turned away as the park reached maximum capacity before 9:00 a.m.

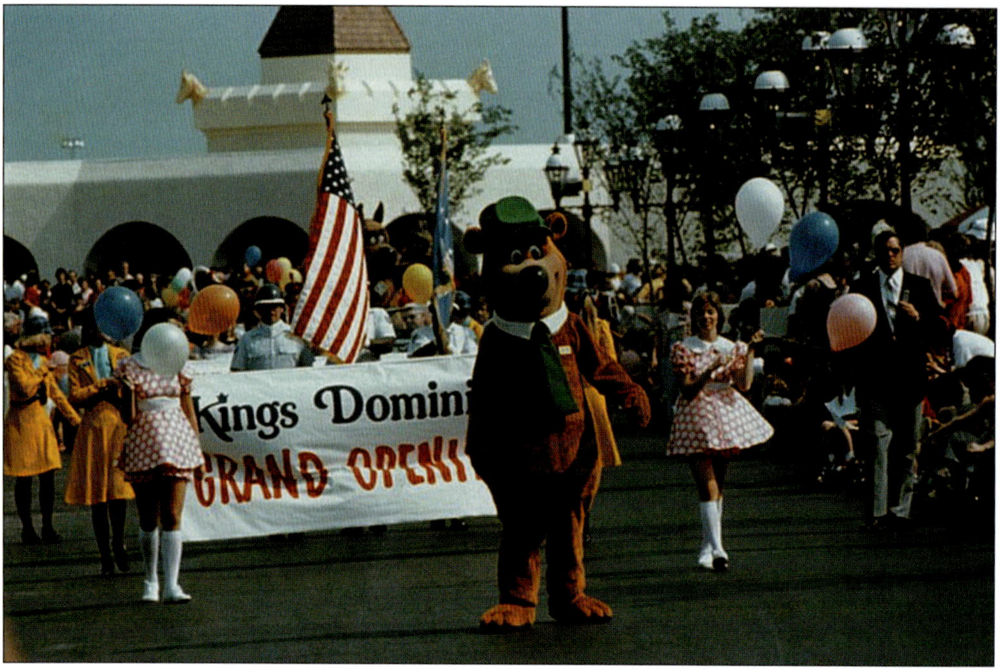

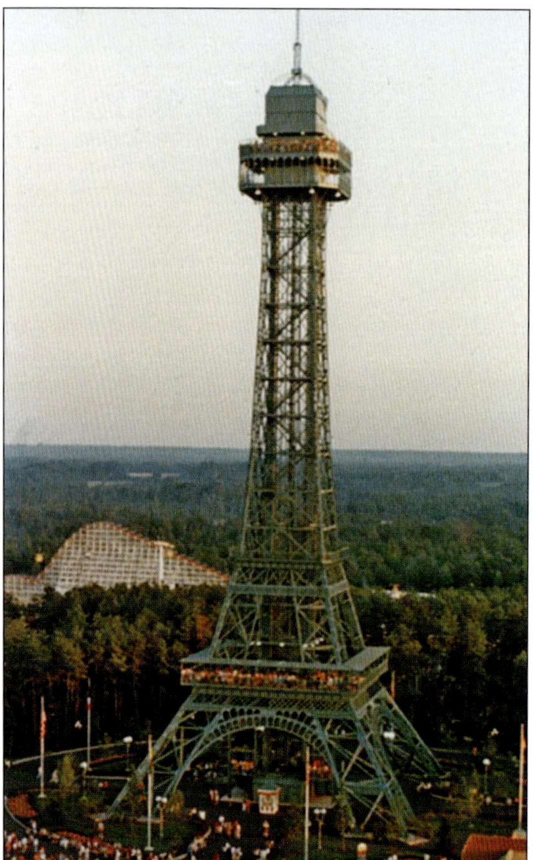

Yogi Bear leads the grand opening parade on Kings Dominion's first official day of operation in the spring of 1975. Other popular Hanna-Barbera costumed characters, such as the Banana Splits, along with park staffers joined in the festivities.

The iconic Eiffel Tower is open for business. Note that the steel structure has now been painted the more familiar dark emerald green. Shown here, guests were permitted to visit the lower observation deck that was situated approximately 50 feet above the ground. High-speed lifts supplied by Haushahn Elevator of Austria each accommodated 50 guests and took 30 seconds to reach the upper deck.

The Rebel Yell wooden roller coaster was the largest thrill ride that debuted during Kings Dominion's opening season. Standing 85 feet tall, the coaster featured two 3,368-foot-long mirror-image tracks that presented a striking profile along the shores of Lake Charles.

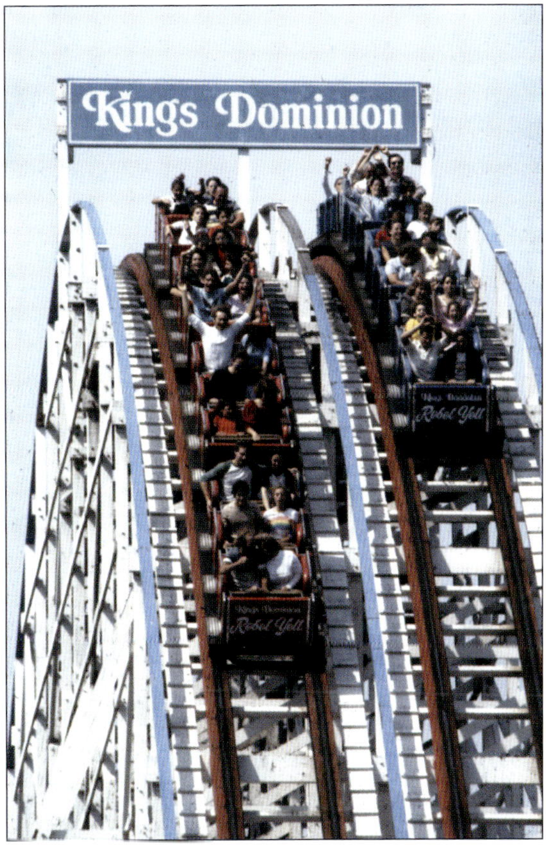

This view captures riders about to experience Rebel Yell's steep 50-degree first drop. Once they reach the bottom, eight stories below, they will attain a top speed of approximately 50 miles per hour and be treated to a tour of the layout. Each of the five-car trains seated 30 riders, which meant Rebel Yell could accommodate 1,200 guests per hour. The trains were supplied by the Philadelphia Toboggan Company.

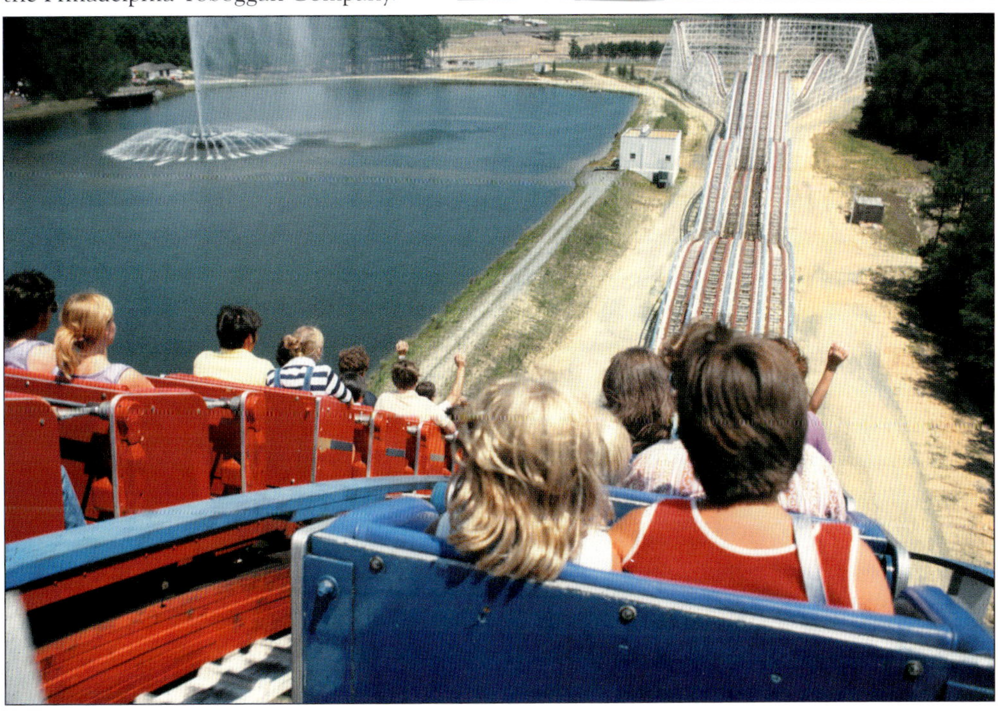

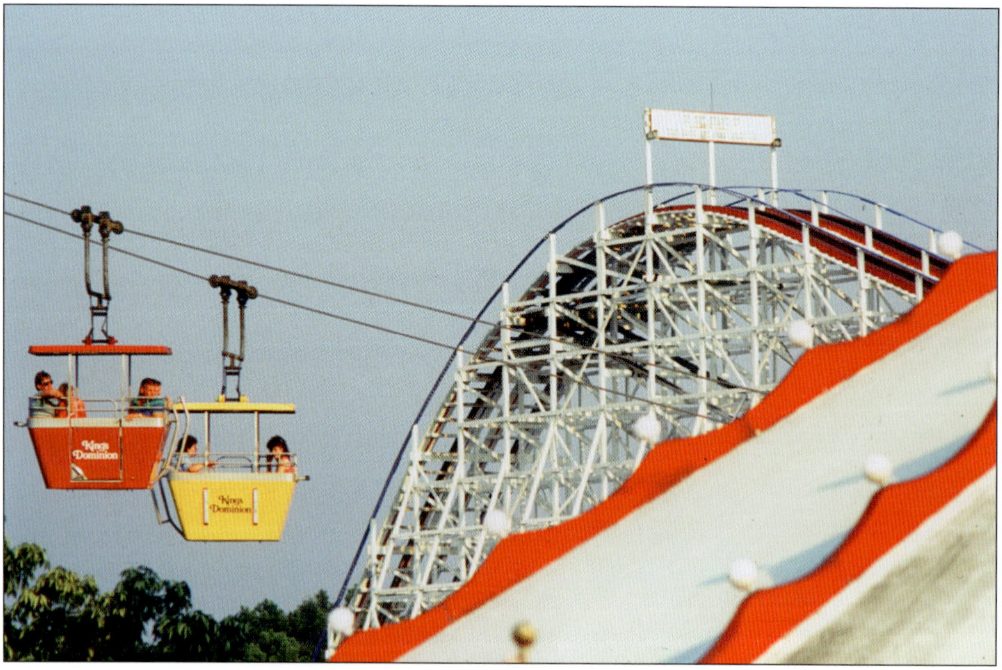

The Sky Ride was a product of Intamin of Switzerland. While mainly a sightseeing attraction, the Sky Ride offered guests a leisurely trip up and over the Coney Island midway. Featuring 36 colorful gondolas, the Sky Ride had two stations: one near Rebel Yell (the "tension" side, named for its job of keeping the suspended cable taut) and the other in Lion Country Safari (the "drive" side, where the ride's massive motor was located).

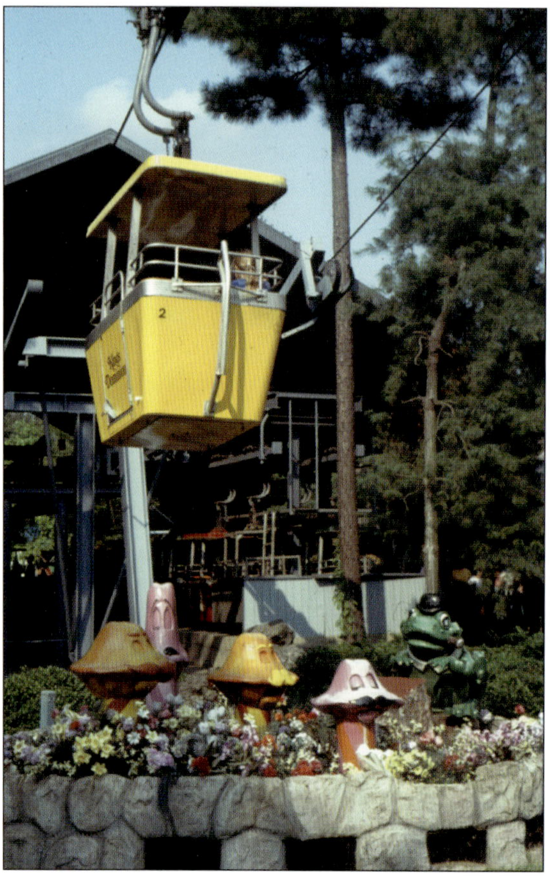

Here, guests arriving or departing the Sky Ride's drive side station are serenaded by the lovable Singing Mushrooms. Lead by a cigar-chomping frog, this harmonic group periodically belted out old-time barbershop quartet tunes. The Sky Ride elevated guests 80 feet into the air along the 250-yard-long flight and offered spectacular views of Coney Island and Lake Charles.

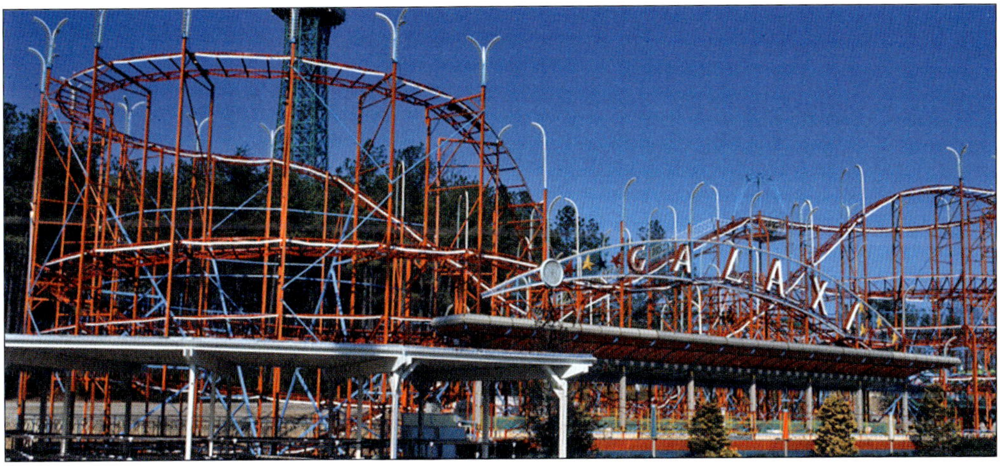

The Galaxi was Kings Dominion's first steel roller coaster. Situated in Candy Apple Grove, it was a popular model supplied by Italian manufacturer SDC. The ride stood approximately 50 feet tall and was characterized by several drops and a number of tight spirals.

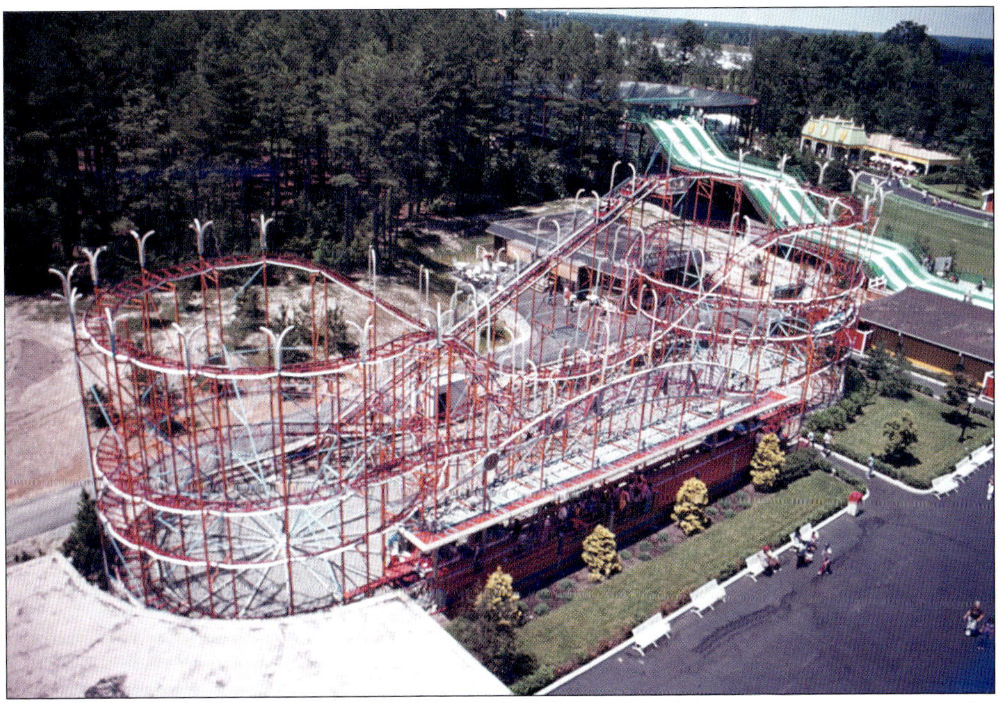

Snapped from the Sky Ride, this shot of the Galaxi shows one of the two-car trains nearing the top of the lift hill while another is barreling through a banked turn about halfway through the course. At far right is another of park's original rides, the Giant Slide.

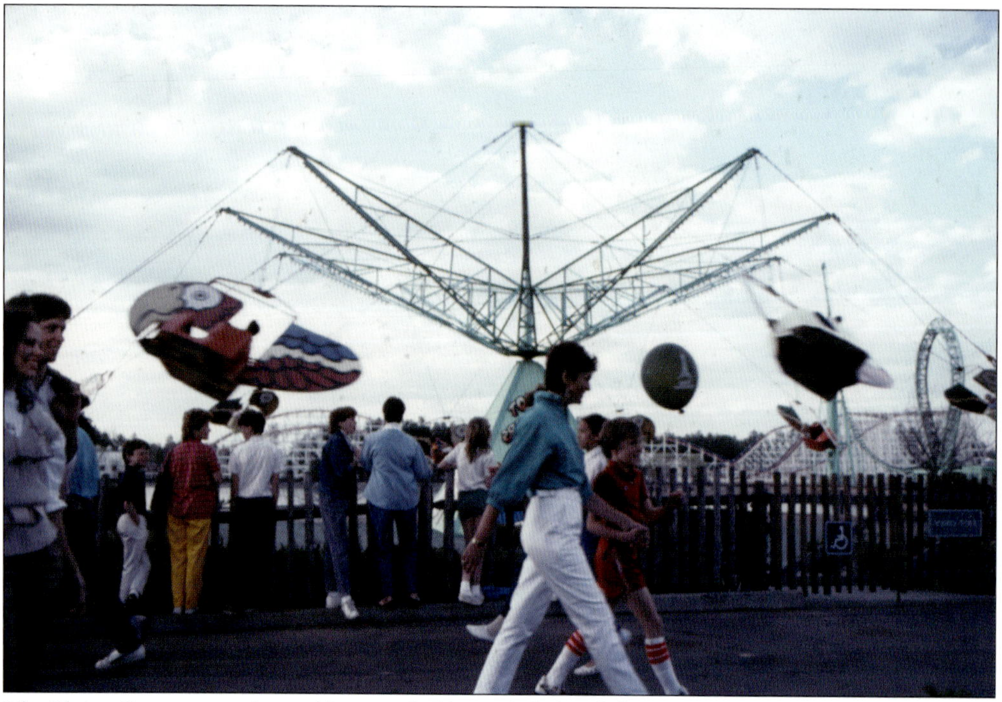

The Flying Scooter was the park's second oldest ride behind the carousel. Built by Chicago's Bisch-Rocco in the 1940s, the Flying Scooter was purchased from New Orleans's closed Pontchartrain Beach Park. It would initially be located in the park's Coney Island area before being moved and renamed several times.

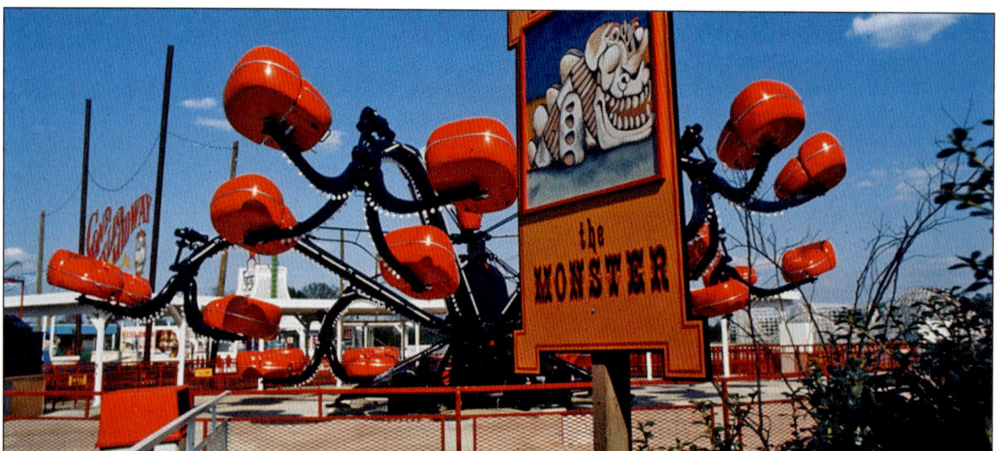

Another ride popular on the traveling fair circuit was Kings Dominion's Monster (also known as the Bad Apple), which was built by the Eyerly Aircraft Company of Oregon. This model, the largest of its kind, treated guests to a whirling, dipping motion while the entire contraption rotated counter-clockwise.

The Wave Swinger is another popular family ride that has been around for many years. Located in Coney Island, Kings Dominion's version was supplied by Zierer of Germany. It features individual open-air chairs suspended from chains. Riders were lifted to a height of approximately 30 feet and treated to a sweeping wave motion as the machine rotated.

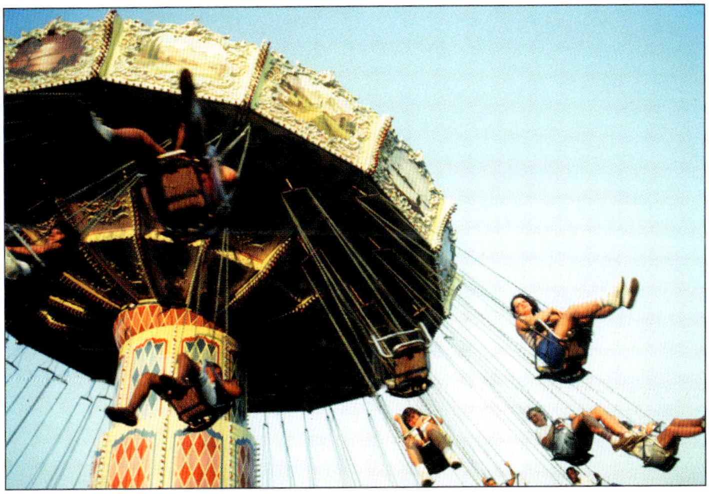

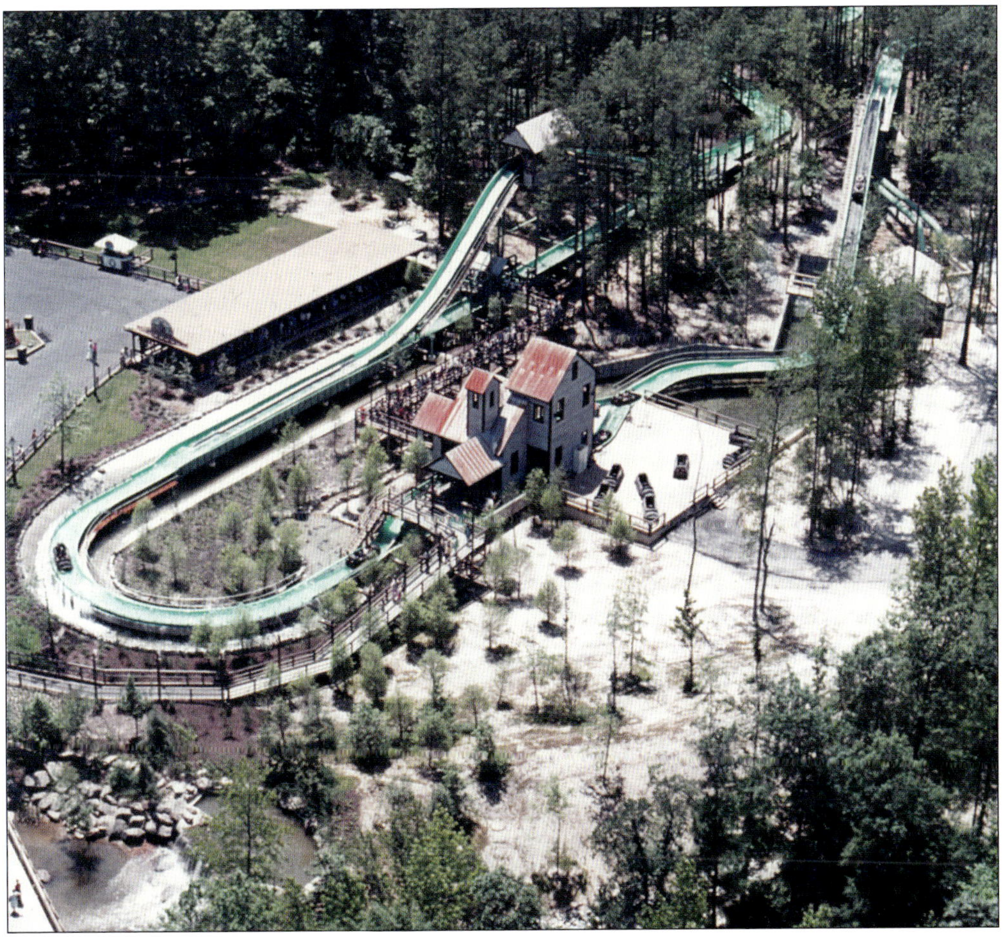

The Shenandoah Lumber Company log flume was built by the California-based Arrow Development Company. Multi-passenger logs were hauled to the highest points via conveyor belts and then preceded to float by gravity through a fiberglass trough. The ride concluded with an exhilarating 40-foot plunge and resulting splashdown.

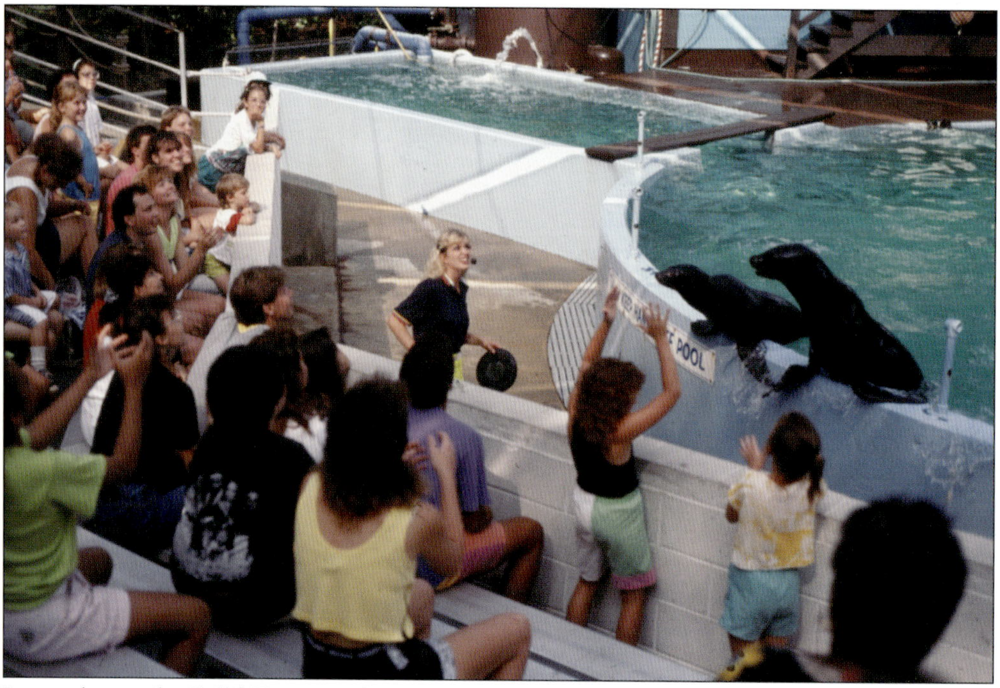

Located near the Eiffel Tower at the entrance to Coney Island, Moby's Seaside Review was a light-hearted aquatics animal show presented several times daily within the confines of an outdoor amphitheater with a stage and large pool at its center.

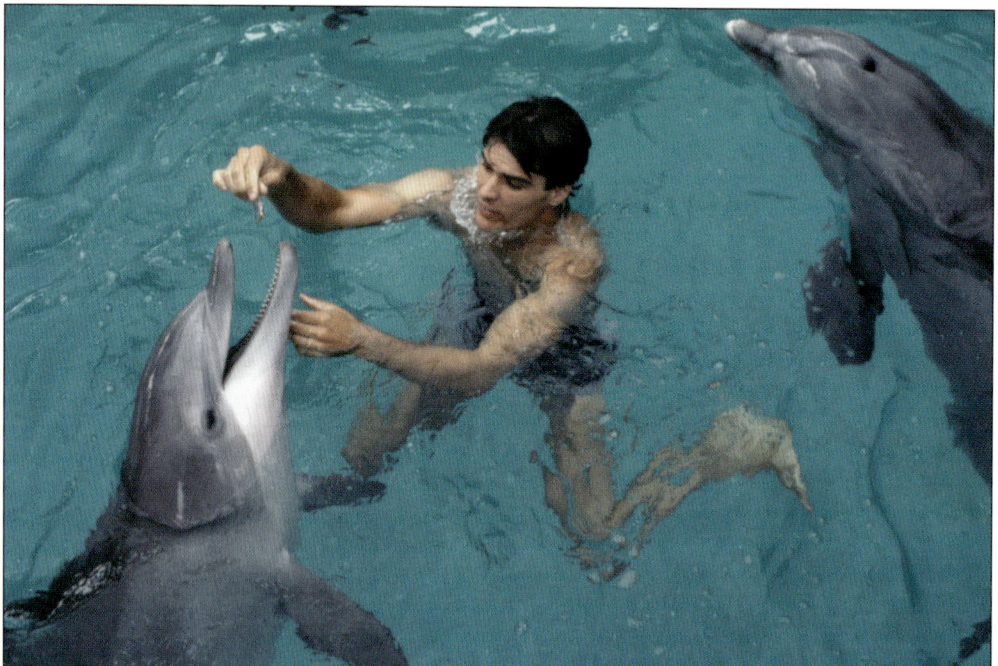

Moby's Seaside Review featured a number of dolphins and sea lions. Like the trainers and specialists based next door in Lion Country Safari, the Kings Dominion employees who worked with these aquatic animals were professionals in their field.

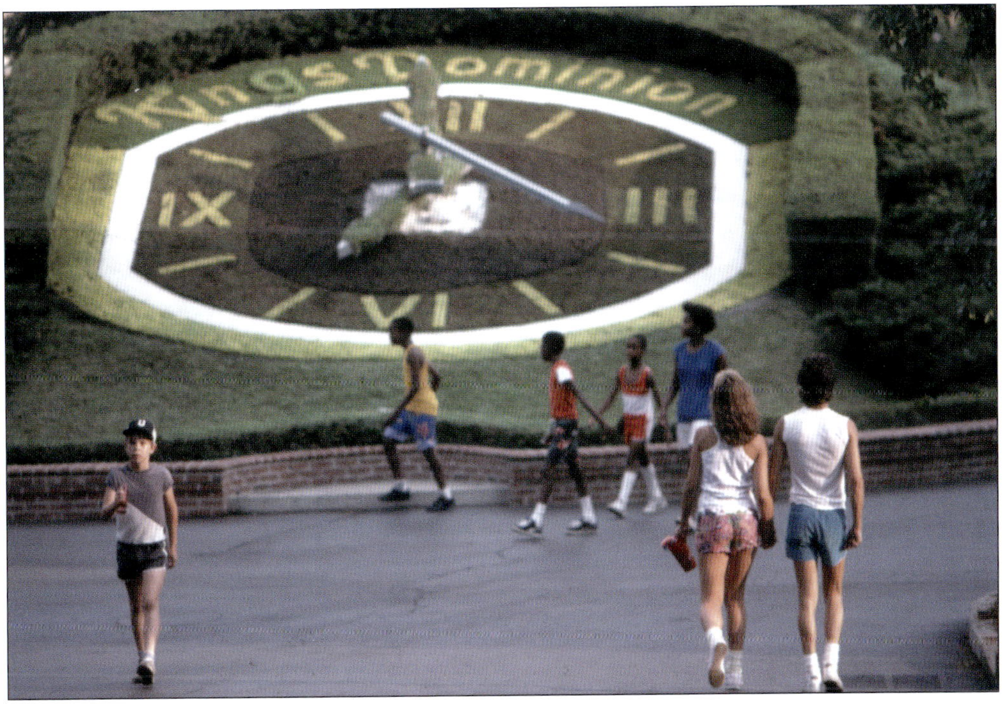

The Floral Clock (pictured here) was a large working timepiece that fit perfectly into its surroundings. Like the Eiffel Tower, the Floral Clock was often used as a meeting place for families and groups. It was located near the carousel on the edge of Coney Island.

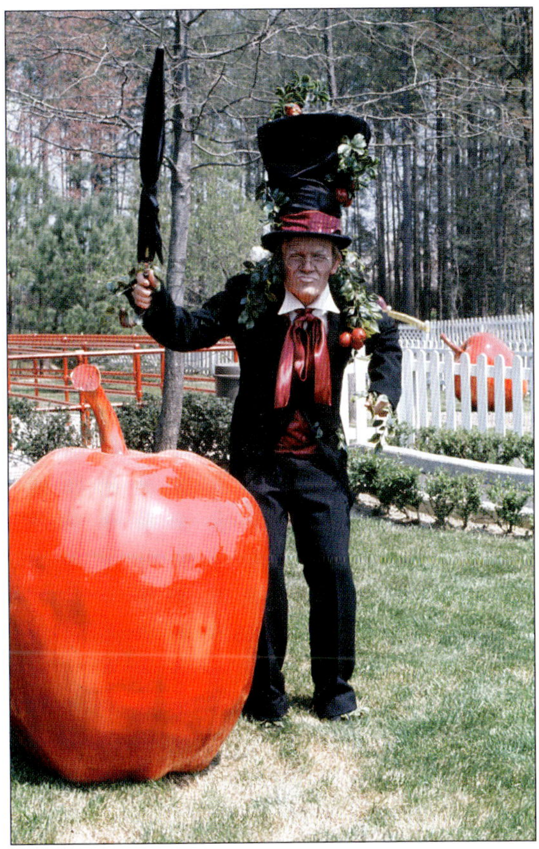

Along with strolling cartoon characters, Kings Dominion also had its share of originals. Here, beside one of the many larger-than-life apples that could be found throughout the Coney Island midway, is Crabby Appleton, played by Mark Krumme, Kings Dominion's director of design.

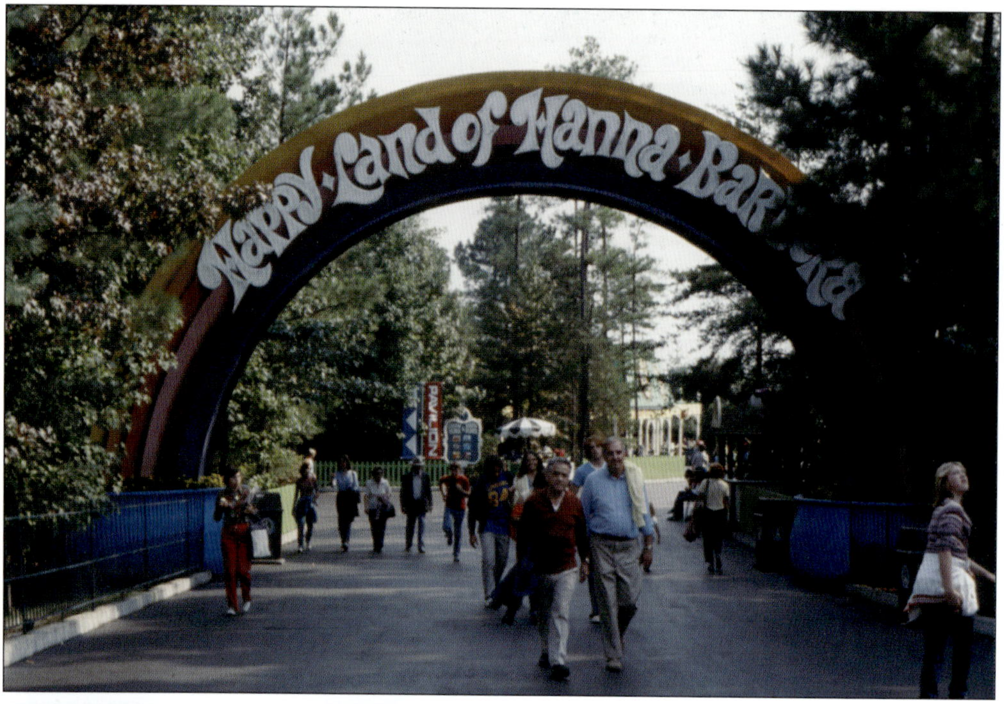

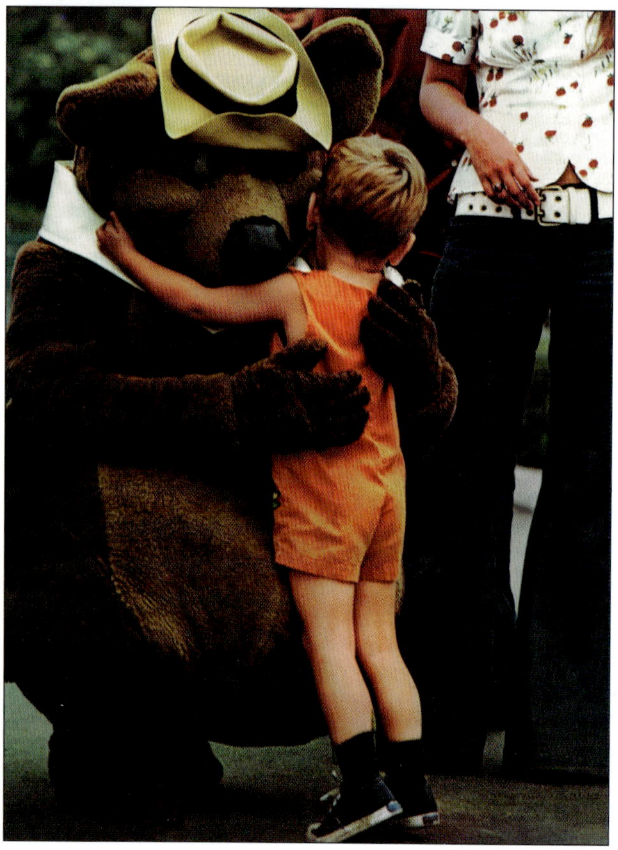

This colorful rainbow arch served as the gateway to the Happy Land of Hanna-Barbera. It promised that once guests passed through the portal they would be transported to a place for the young and young-at-heart

For Kings Dominion's younger guests, seeing their favorite cartoon characters come to life was a highlight of a park visit. Memories like this one were made on a daily basis at Kings Dominion.

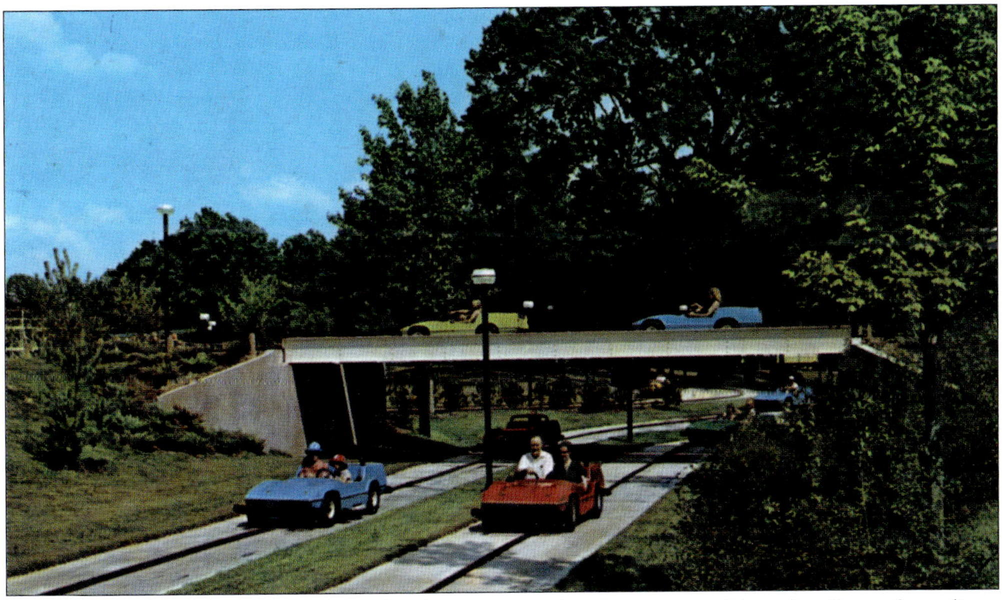

This postcard view shows Wacky Wheels, an auto ride where guests "drove" a fleet of gasoline-powered convertibles along a winding concrete roadway in the Happy Land of Hanna-Barbera. A central guide rail in each lane made sure that motorists remained on the road. Arrow Development supplied the Wacky Wheels.

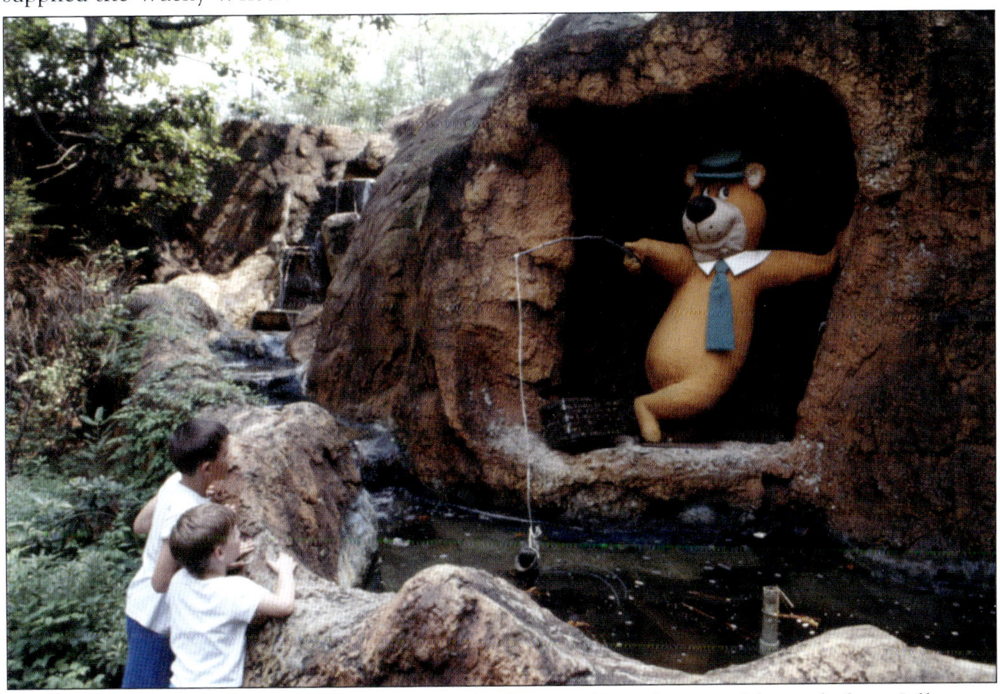

Yogi's Cave was a self-guided walk through the home of Yogi Bear and his pals from Jellystone Park. The cave walls were adorned with glowing gems while a waterfall, sing-along with Boo-Boo, and other special effects kept guests entertained as they made their way through the semi-darkness. At the end of the attraction they had to traverse the slanted floor in a tilted cabin that Yogi helped build.

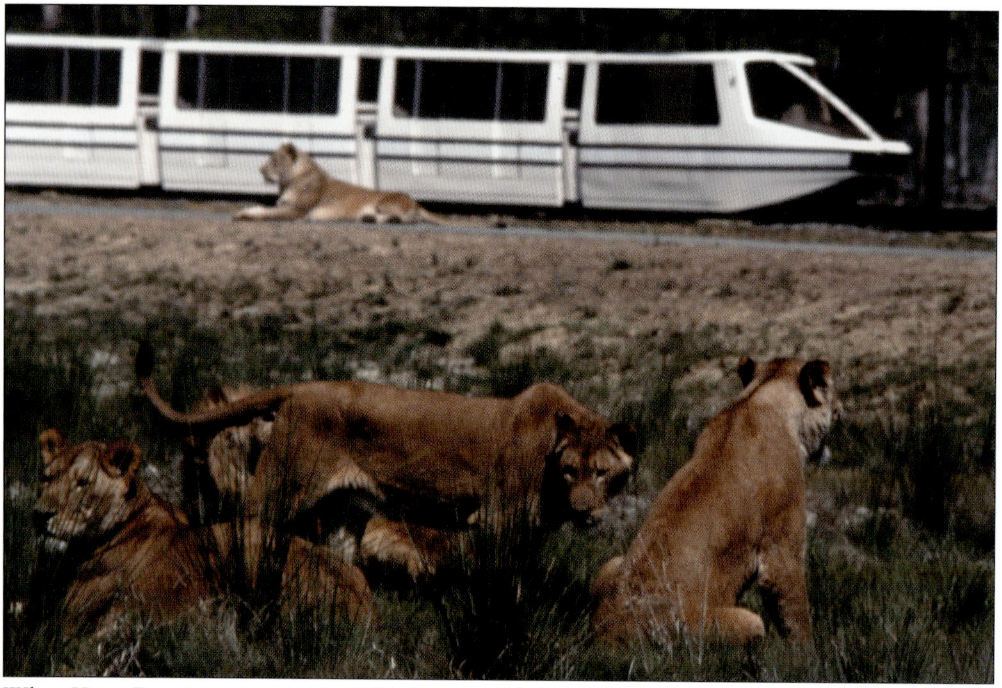

When Kings Dominion opened in 1975, the automobile drive-through aspect of Lion Country Safari was discontinued. In its place was a sleek new conveyance dubbed the Wild Animal Safari Monorail. This new monorail allowed guests to enjoy viewing the animals in air-conditioned comfort.

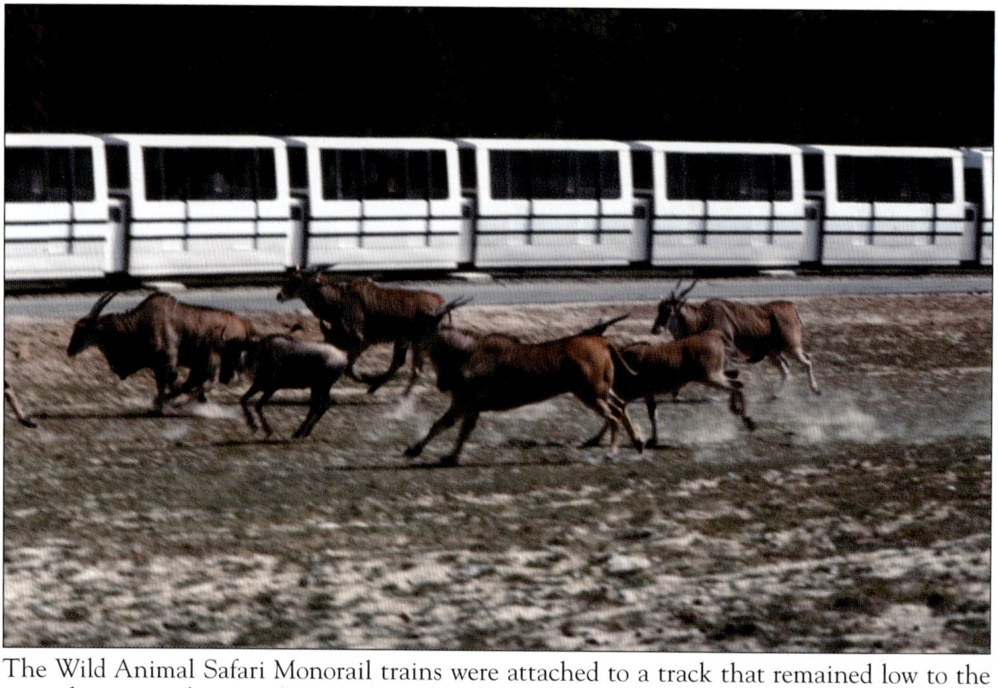

The Wild Animal Safari Monorail trains were attached to a track that remained low to the ground as it wound its way through the woods and across the savannas that comprised the various habitats. Some of the animals were less stressed by the quiet monorail trains than they had been by the former drivers and their cars.

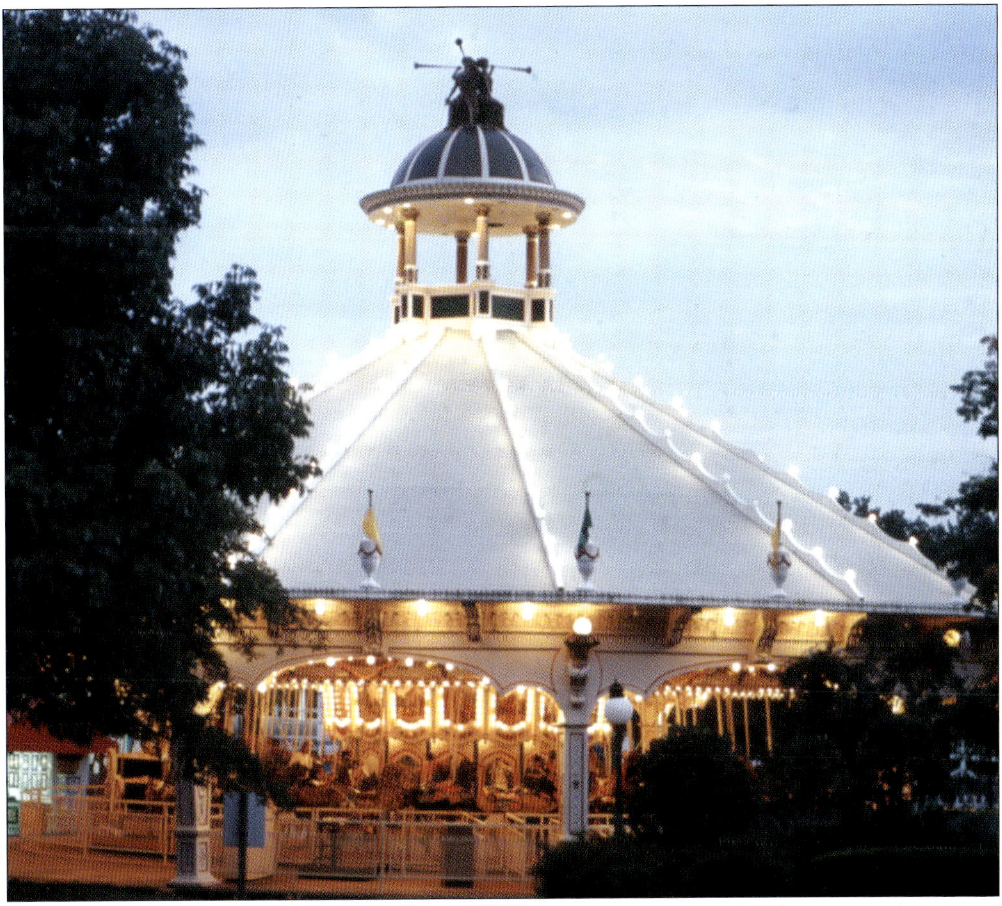

With the arrival of dusk, Kings Dominion begins to exhibit another side of its personality. Here, the carousel's many white incandescent lights lend it a magical fairy-tale appearance.

The Royal Fountain on International Street seems alive with its plumes of glowing water while shops and streets shine with thousands of colorful light bulbs. Neon and other forms of lighting gave the rides a dazzling new perspective.

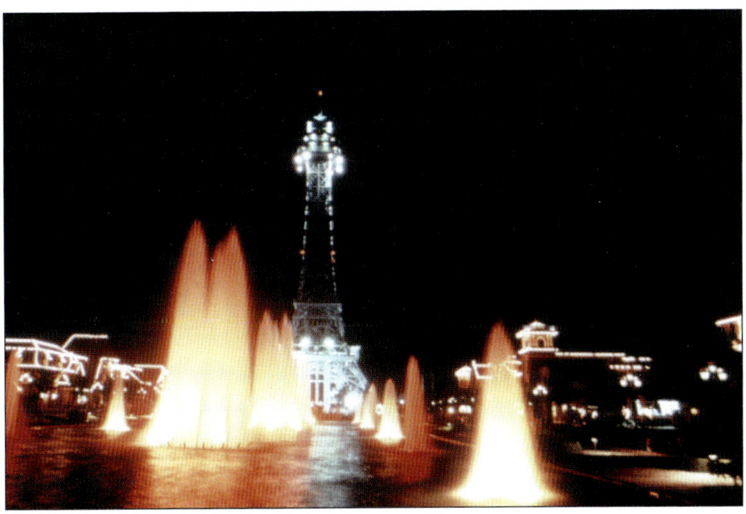

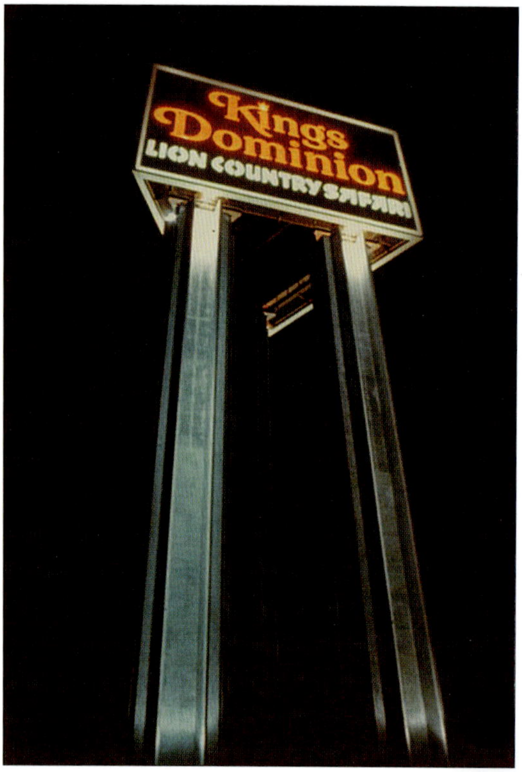

Kings Dominion's impressive first year of operation was more successful than any of its creators could possibly have imagined. More than 1.5 million visitors passed through the gates. These evening images, captured at the end of that 1975 season, show both the park's towering marquis and a spectacular fireworks display behind the Eiffel Tower.

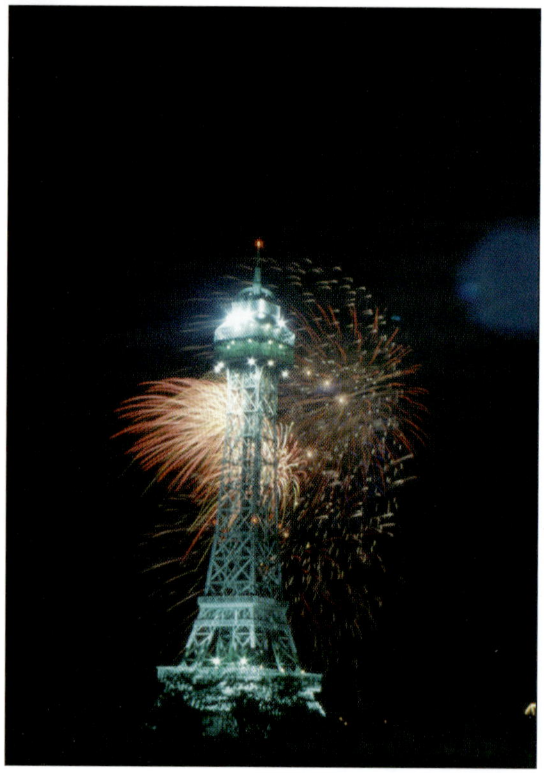

Three

Popularity Spurs Growth

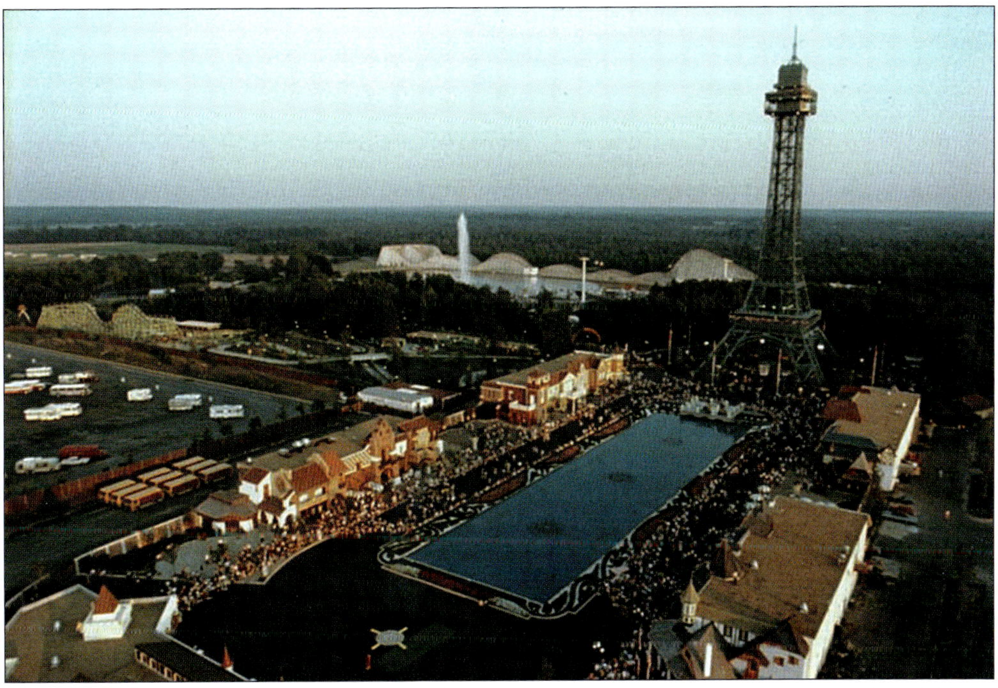

The momentum initiated during Kings Dominion's inaugural year continued unabated for its sophomore season and throughout the remaining decade of the 1970s. In 1976, the park opened with several new rides and attractions. The image here captured in spring 1976 shows a very busy International Street and Eiffel Tower. Major attractions visible in the background are the Scooby-Doo wooden coaster (left) along with the fountain on Lake Charles and Rebel Yell.

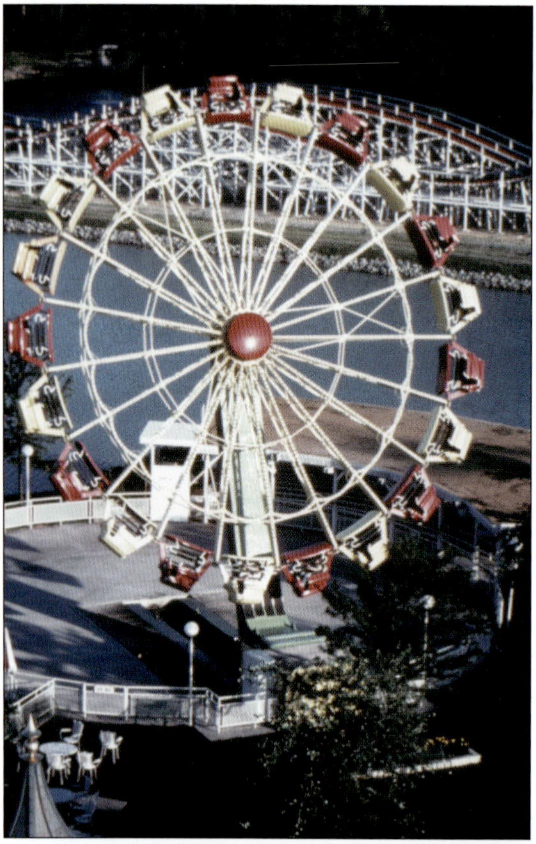

The 1976 season also saw the introduction of a series of new rides. One of the most popular was Apple Turnover. Known by the trade name of Enterprise, the ride was supplied by Anton Schwarzkopf of Germany. After loading flat on the ground with guests boarding two-seat gondolas, it began to rotate at a high speed. A powerful hydraulic arm lifted the spinning wheel into the air at a near-90-degree angle.

Also added during the second season were the Flying Bobs (Matterhorn), Calypso, and Mount Kilimanjaro (pictured here). The latter was a Bayern Kurve from Anton Schwarzkopf, located in Lion Country Safari area. It utilized a train of low-slung vehicles that sped around a circular track in and around a mountain facade that featured a waterfall.

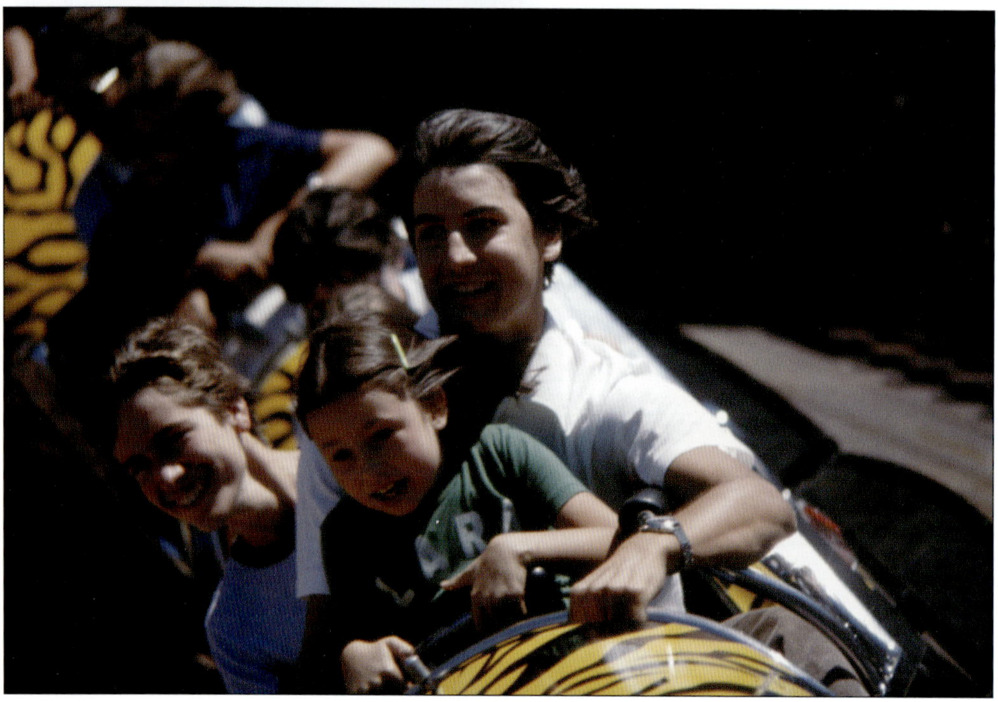

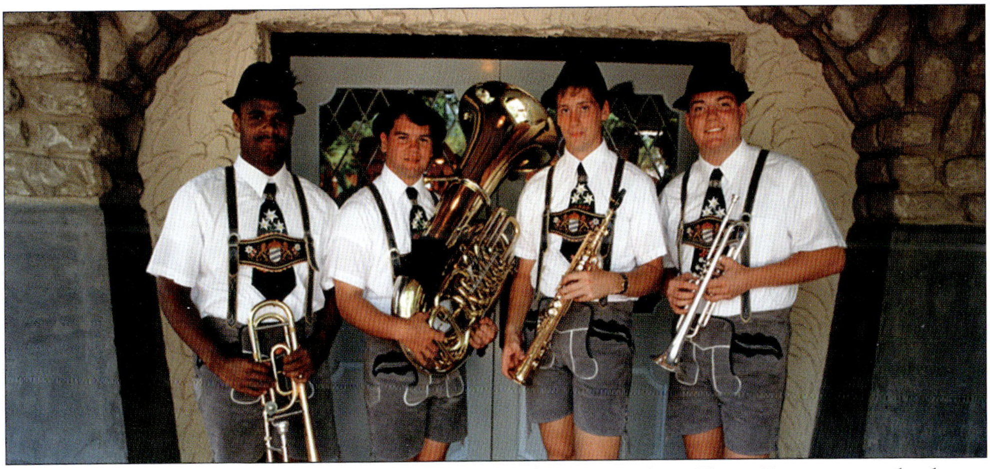

Since the early days, live entertainment has always been a staple at Kings Dominion, whether it be the roving Clown Band, which will be featured later, or this quartet of musicians, outfitted in traditional German attire, that played lively tunes from Germany along International Street.

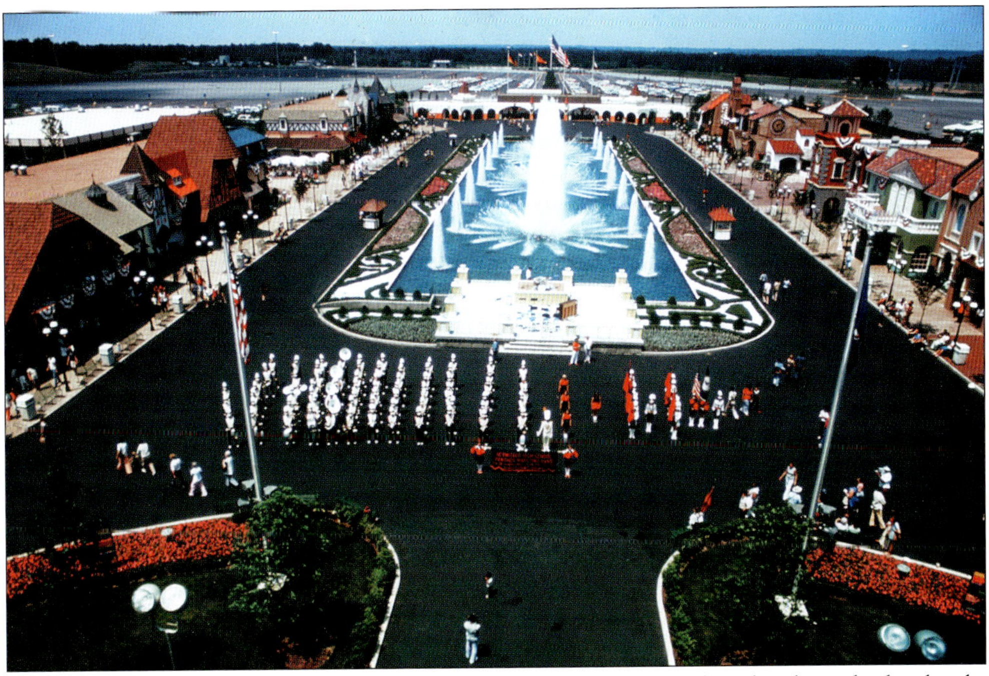

Kings Dominion's live entertainment also consisted of competitions from local area high schools. Here, the Hermitage High School Panther Marching Band lines up in formation.

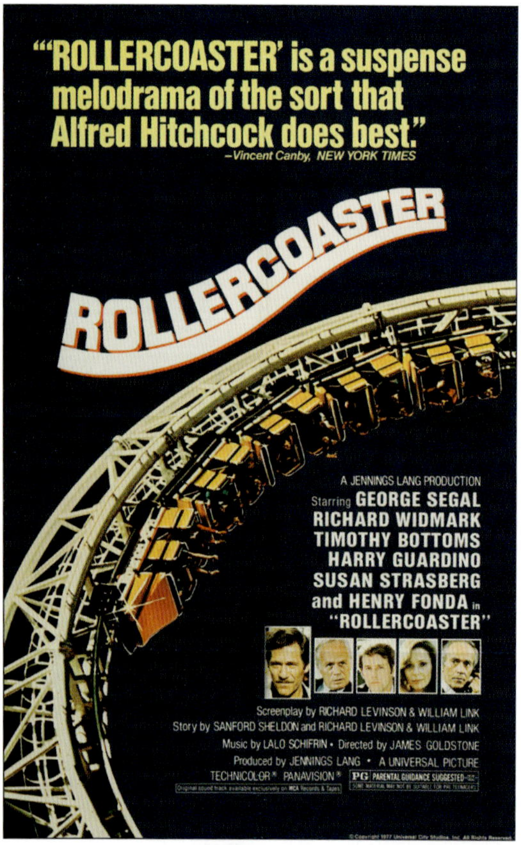

It was also during the 1976 season that Kings Dominion became a Hollywood darling thanks to the park serving as a major filming location for Universal's 1977 release of *Rollercoaster*. Kings Dominion's general manager Dennis Speigel (and the author of this book's foreword) had a cameo in the film as the park's general manager.

To promote the film *Rollercoaster*, a coaster-riding marathon was arranged in early 1977. Die-hard coaster fans and professional marathoners descended on Kings Dominion with the intent of outlasting each other as Rebel Yell operated constantly. In the front seat are actor George Segal, film producer Jennings Lang, and the park's general manager, Dennis Speigel. (Courtesy Richard Munch.)

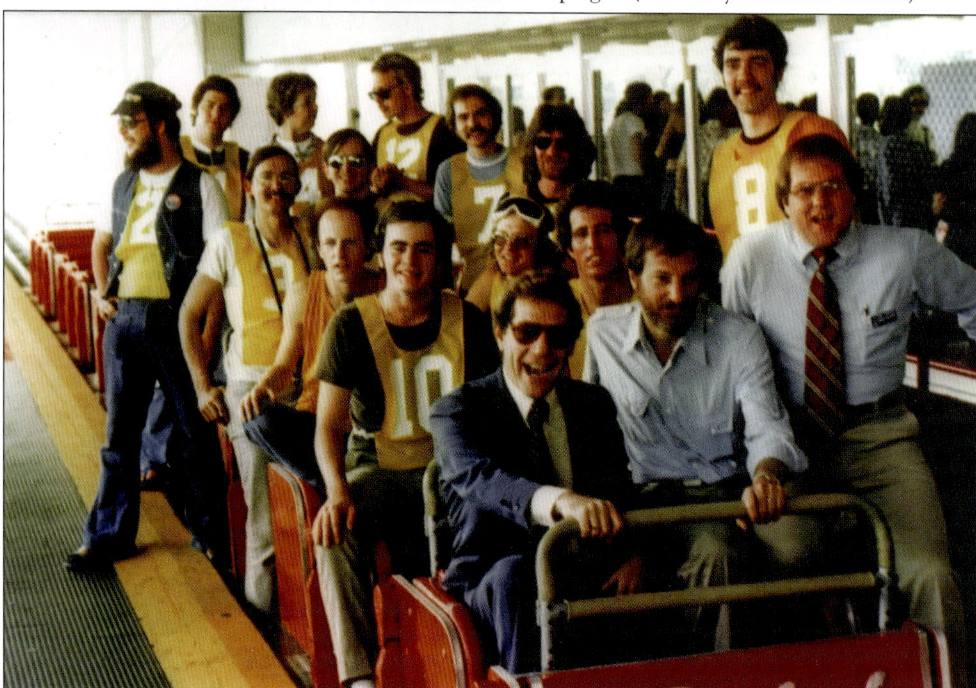

And then there were only four remaining marathon participants. With temperatures plunging to near-freezing at night, many dropped out after only a few hours. Here, a lone Rebel Yell train plunges down the first drop during the event. The winner was Noel Aube, who managed to last 101 hours. (Courtesy Richard Munch.)

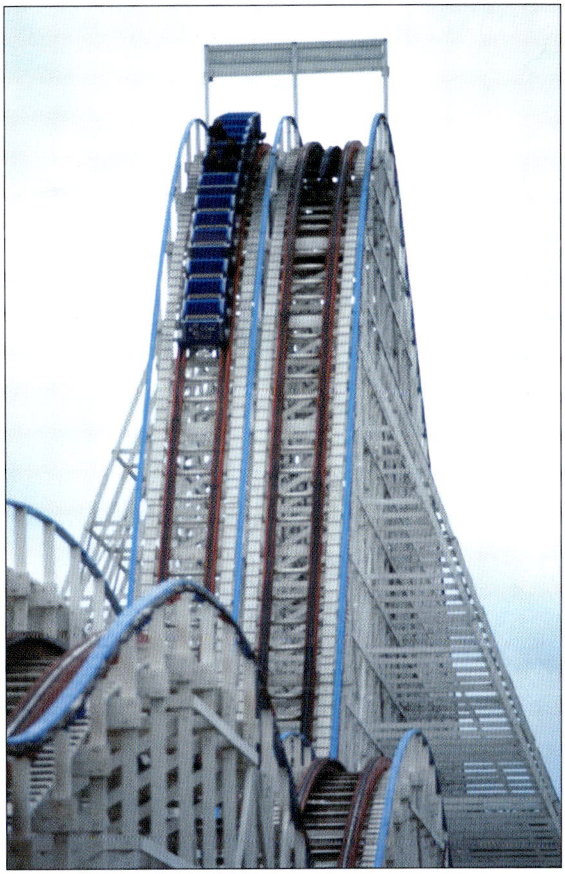

During the marathon, three participants and coaster fans—Richard Munch (pictured here with a Rebel Yell train on the transfer track), Paul Greenwald, and Roy Brashears—laid the foundation for the American Coaster Enthusiasts (ACE). Their 8,000 members are dedicated to the enjoyment, historical importance, and preservation of roller coasters worldwide. (Courtesy Richard Munch.)

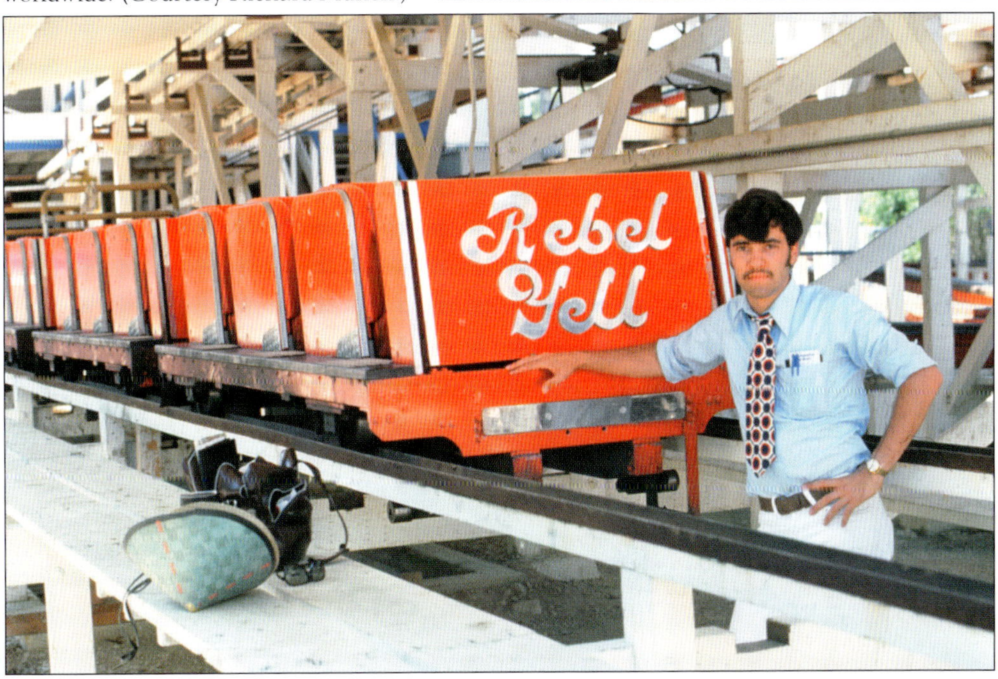

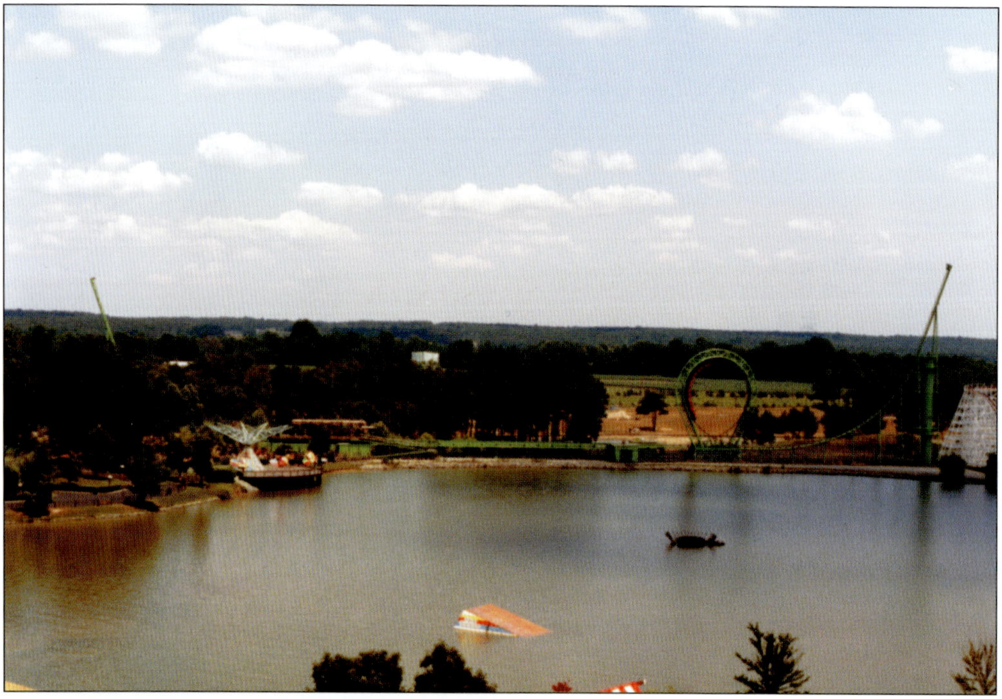

In 1977, Kings Dominion introduced King Kobra, its most innovative new roller coaster to date. King Kobra offered a ride experience unlike any other. This view shows the entire layout of King Kobra, with Lake Charles in the foreground. (Courtesy Gary Slade.)

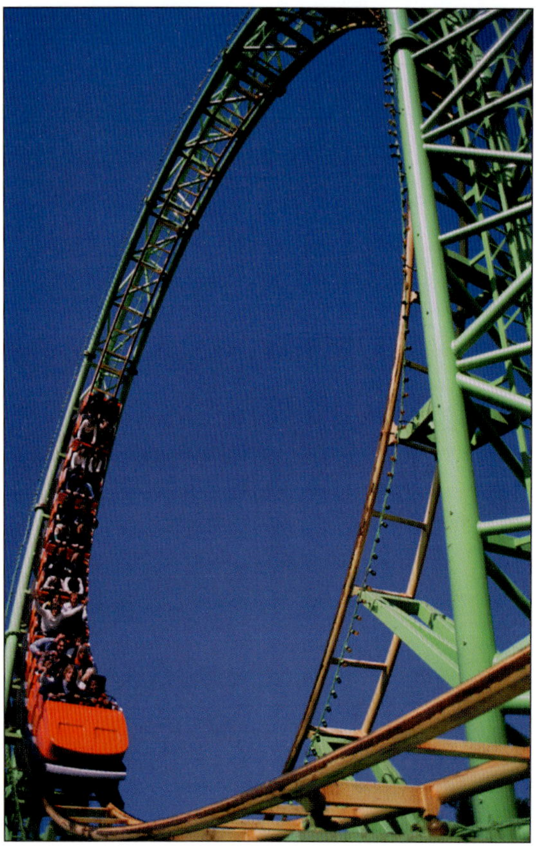

A product of Germans Anton Schwarzkopf and Werner Stengel, King Kobra featured a seven-car, 28-passenger train, which was launched out of the station from 0 to 53 miles per hour in a matter of seconds. The ride included a 46-foot-diameter vertical loop followed by a 13-story, 70-degree ascent. Once at the top, riders were momentarily weightless as the train stalled and then rolled backwards.

After negotiating the loop in reverse, the train roared through the station and up a steep reverse spike of track. Stalling once more, it then rolled into the boarding platform, where it came to a halt. (Courtesy Gary Slade.)

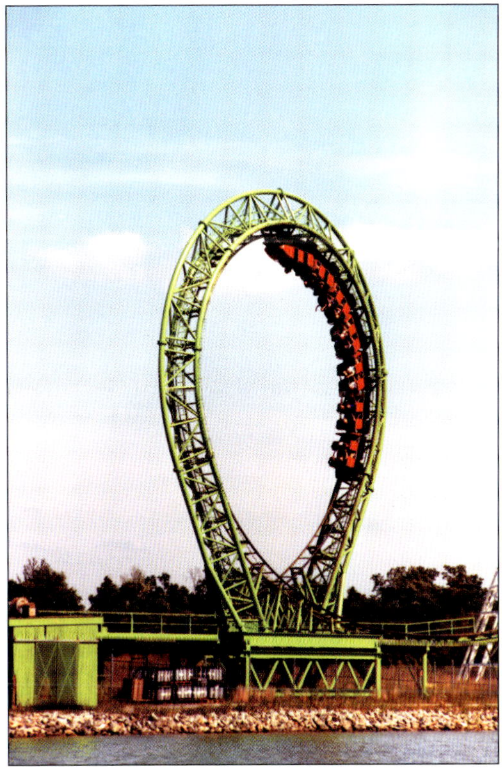

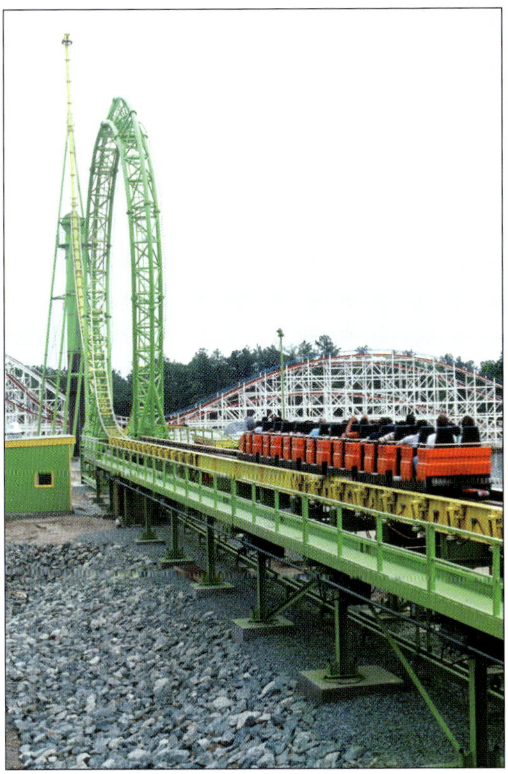

King Kobra's state-of-the-art launch was accomplished mechanically via a cable attached to a 40-ton weight enclosed with a hollow steel silo beneath the forward track spike. A cable stretching from this weight was in turn connected to a "pusher" that made contact with the train (visible here behind the last car). (Courtesy Richard Munch.)

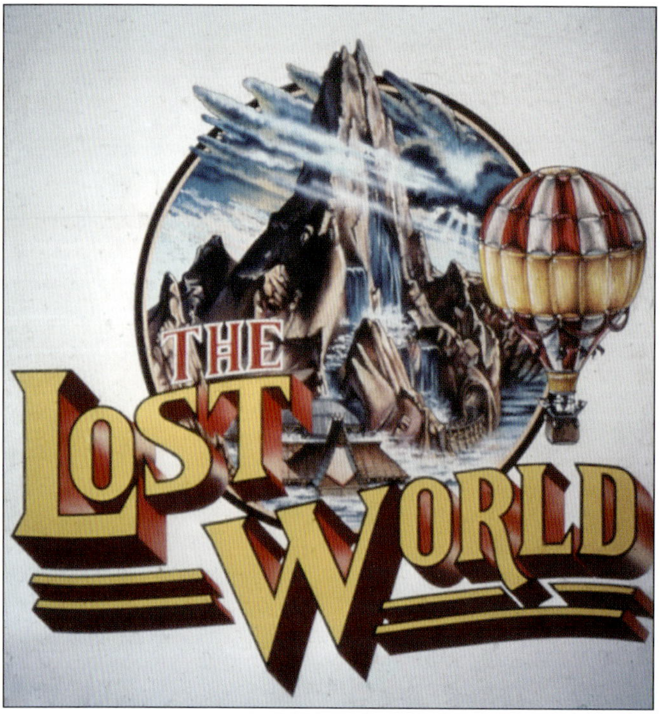

Kings Dominion's 1978 season would be remembered for the addition of its own campground, but it was also when the park began construction on its most expensive attraction (over $20 million) since its opening—the Lost World. The 170-foot-tall "mountain" housed three attractions: Time Shaft (Rotor), Voyage to Atlantis (boat ride), and Journey to the Land of Dooz (themed mine train).

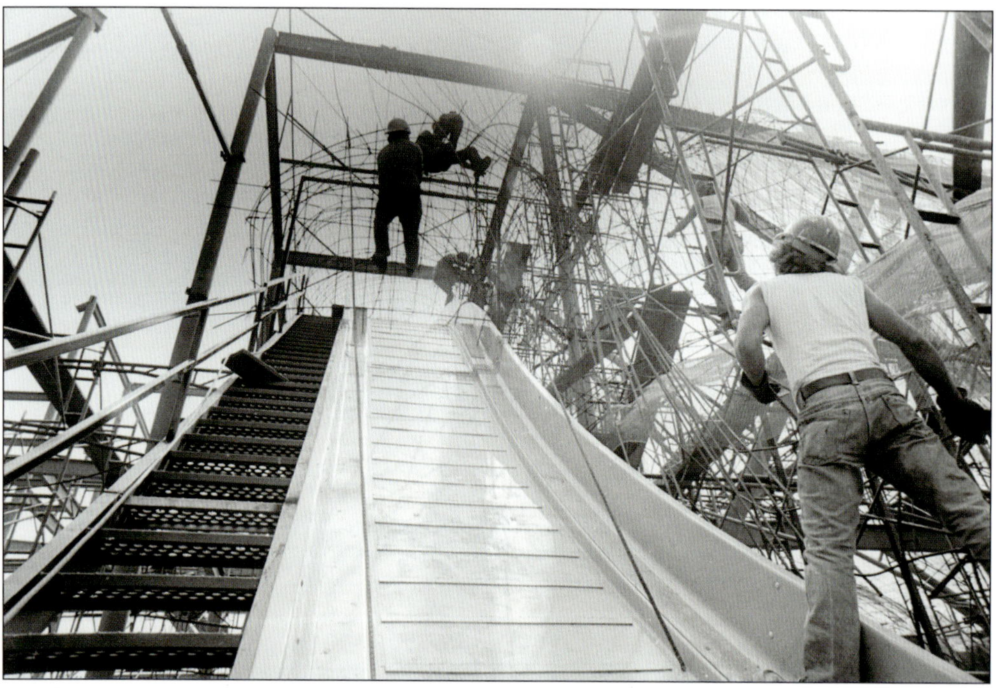

Building the Lost World proved to be a formidable endeavor for the contractors as the mountain was comprised of several tons of steel I-beams, wire mesh, and concrete. In this image, workers labor to connect the mesh, over which a layer of concrete will be applied to create the mountain's rocky exterior. The ramp in the center is the trough through which speeding boats would travel to the splashdown for Voyage to Atlantis.

The ride used standard tubular roller coaster tracks and a chain lift to haul the trains to the ride's highest section. Once they reached the top, onboard motors moved the trains through the course and back down to the boarding on the lower level.

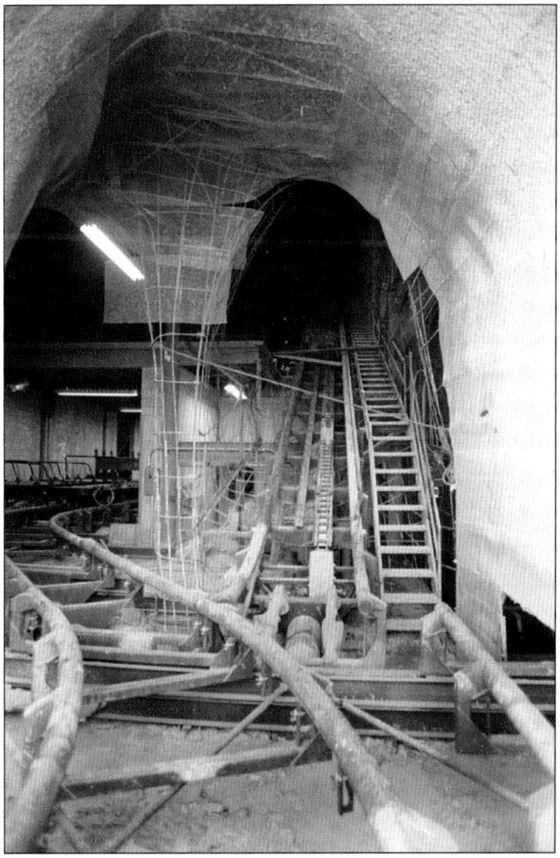

Journey to the Land of Dooz was a powered mine train supplied by Arrow Development. The ride would begin deep inside the mountain with guests boarding one of the four-car trains (two are pictured here on their storage tracks near the station).

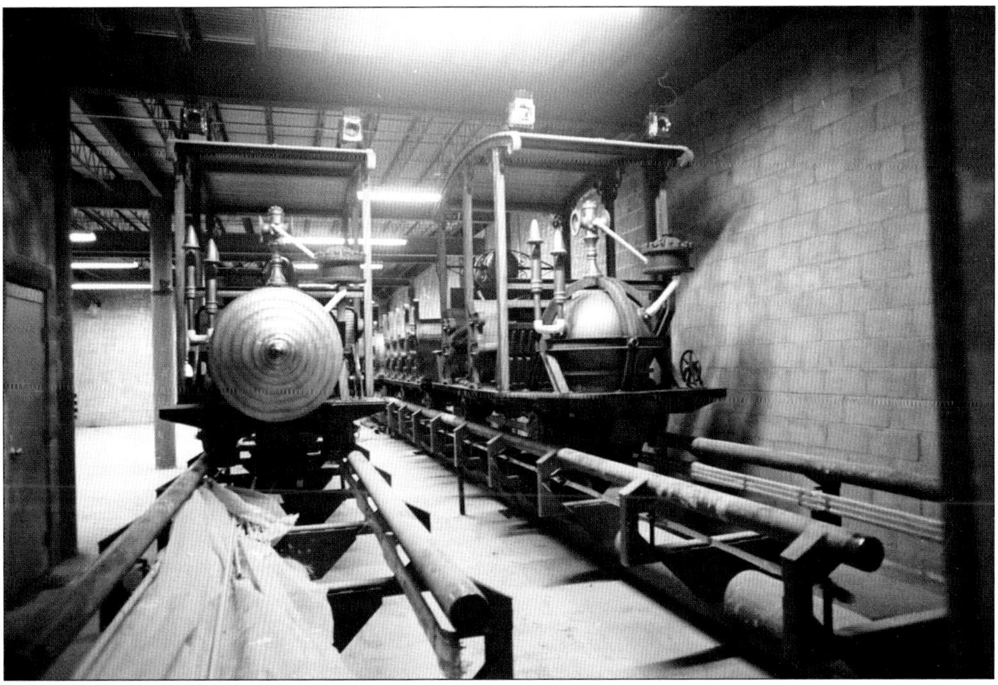

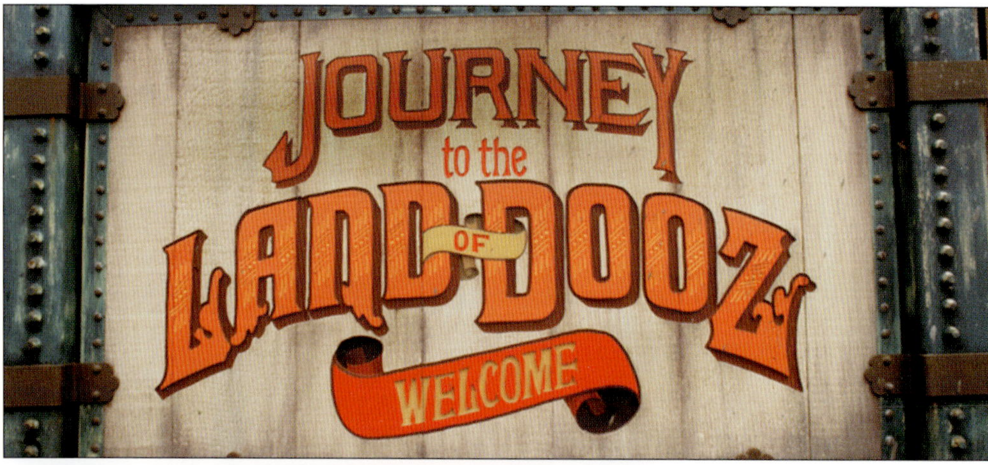

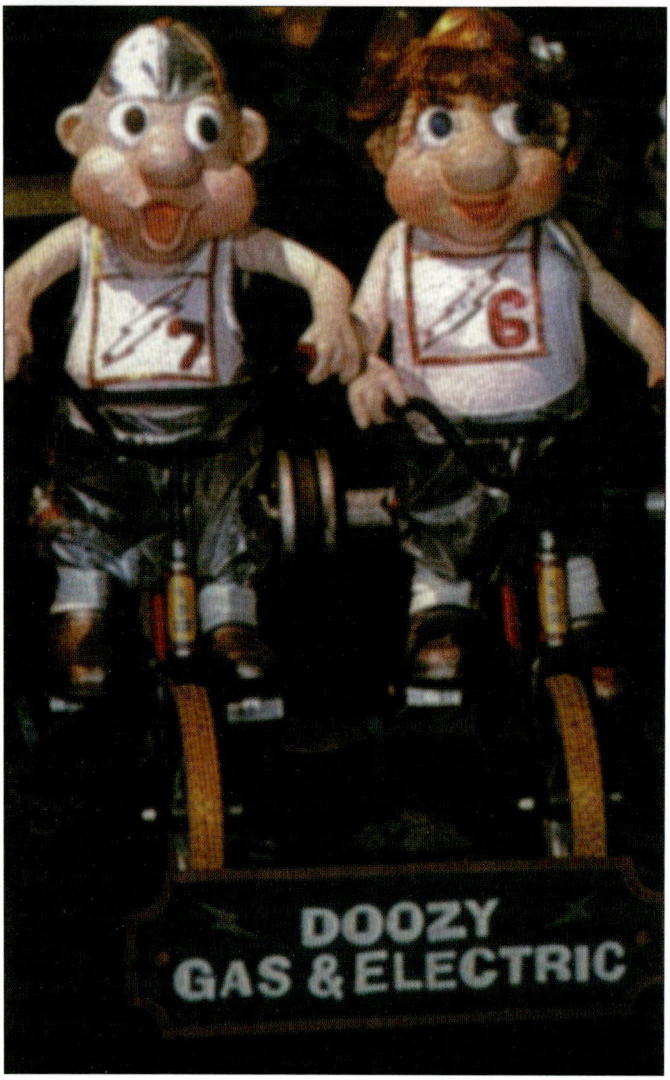

While the above photograph shows the entrance to Journey to the Land of Dooz, the shot at left depicts some of what guests would see during the trip. They would discover that Doozies are "responsible for many things humans take for granted like helping to push flowers and plants out of the ground or manufacturing water and air."

The second major attraction inside the Lost World was an enclosed boat ride supplied by Arrow Development. Six-passenger fiberglass boats floated through several scenes. This image shows the completed mountain with Voyage to Atlantis in operation. (Courtesy Gary Slade.)

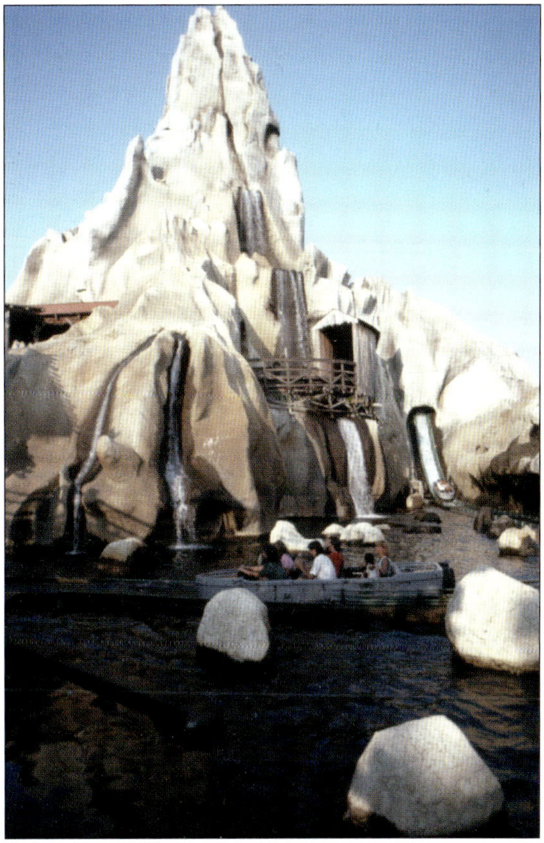

The Voyage to Atlantis theme only lasted a single season. The following year it would be re-themed as The Haunted River with boats traveling through six new scenes. This image, captured from the Eiffel Tower, finds a boat at the top of the 40-foot plunge finale.

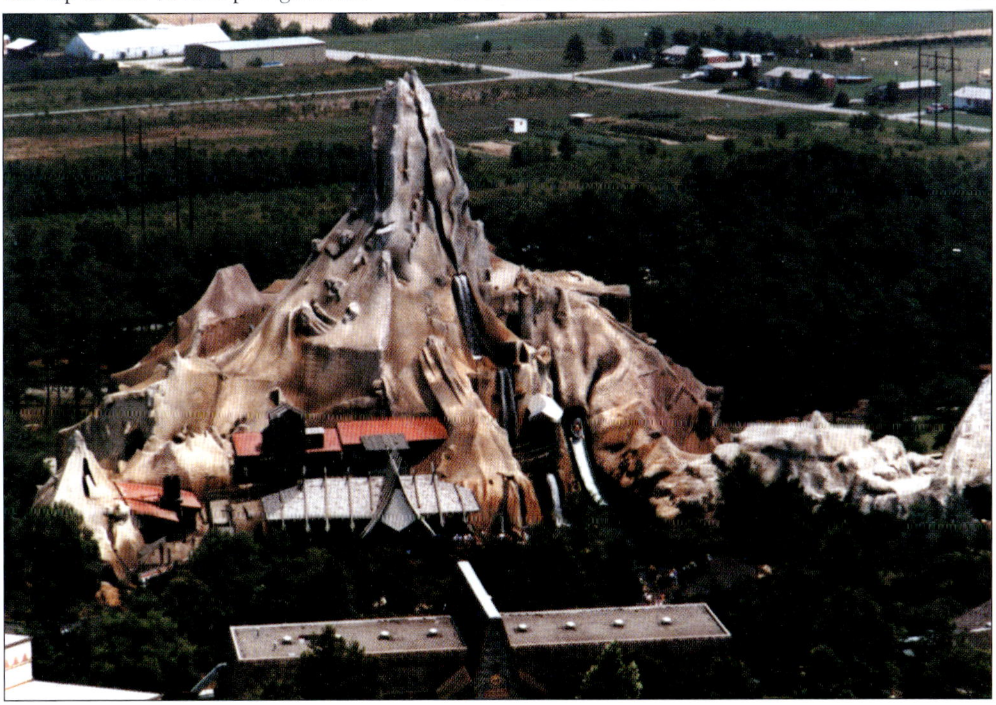

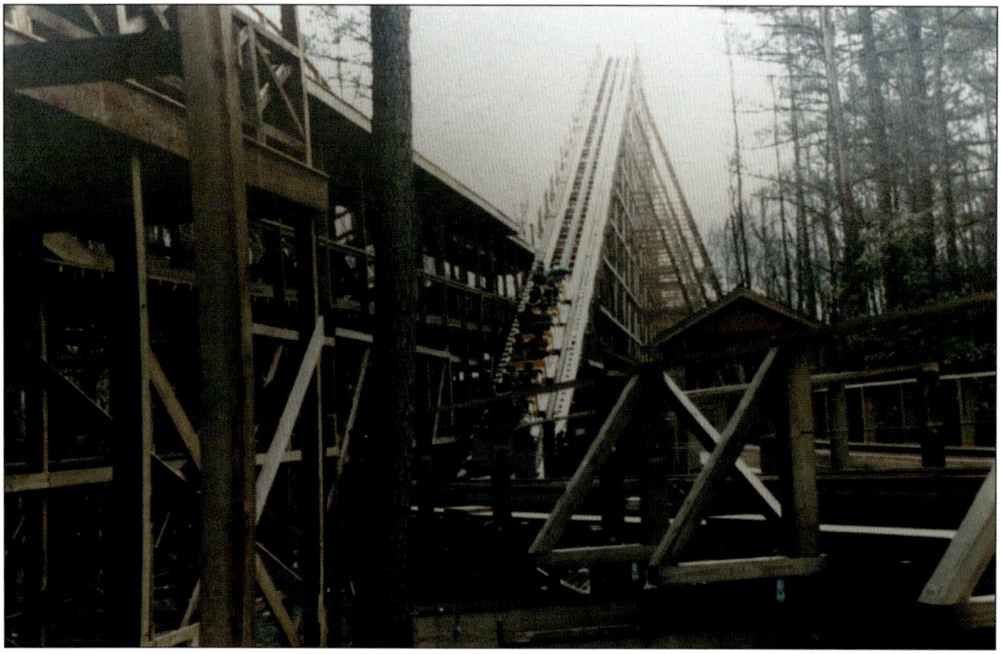

Kings Dominion gave thrill seekers something to scream about in 1982 when it introduced the park's second wooden roller coaster, Grizzly. Anchoring an expansion of the Old Virginia area, Grizzly was inspired by the Wildcat, a classic Philadelphia Toboggan Company–designed coaster that operated at Ohio's Coney Island (1926–1964).

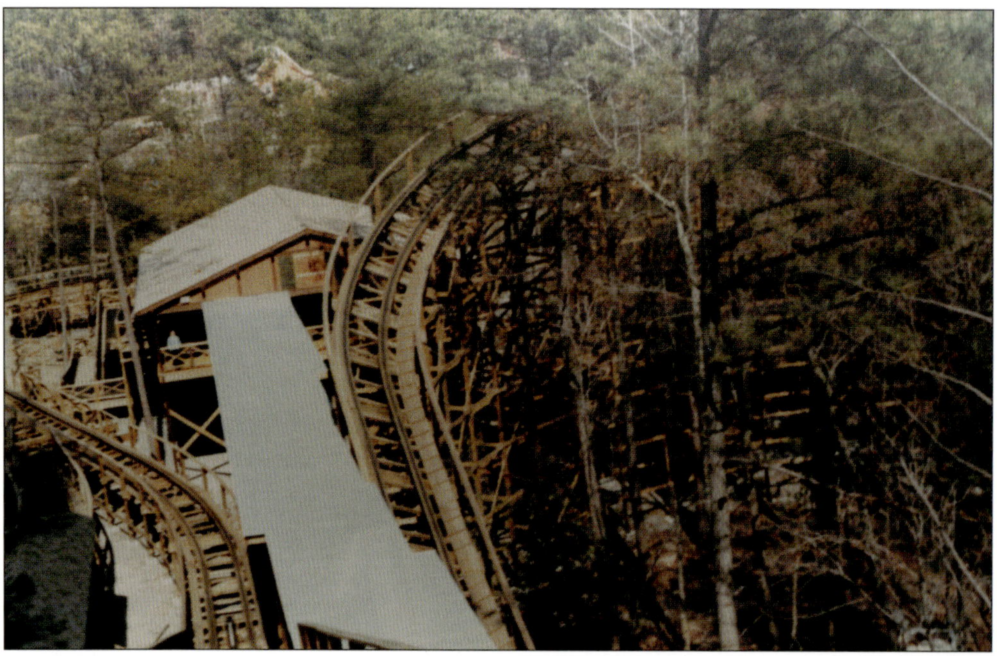

The Grizzly was a true twister. This means that instead of a sprawling, elongated layout, the new coaster was very compact, having drops, numerous track crossovers, and plenty of turns. This angle, captured looking backwards near the crest of the 87-foot-tall lift hill, shows the coaster's station in the center and the approach into the fan turn, halfway through the 3,150-foot-long course.

Like Rebel Yell, Grizzly featured trains supplied by PTC. This point-of-view action shot, taken on opening day in 1982, reveals one of the new coaster's most intimidating secrets: a high-speed dive into a dark tunnel that contains a hidden, air-time filled speed bump. This raucous element has endeared Grizzly to coaster fans ever since.

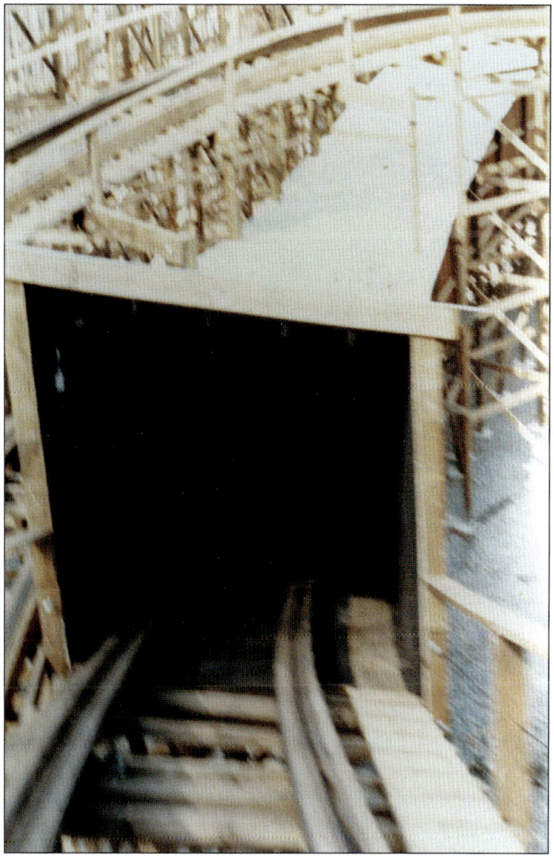

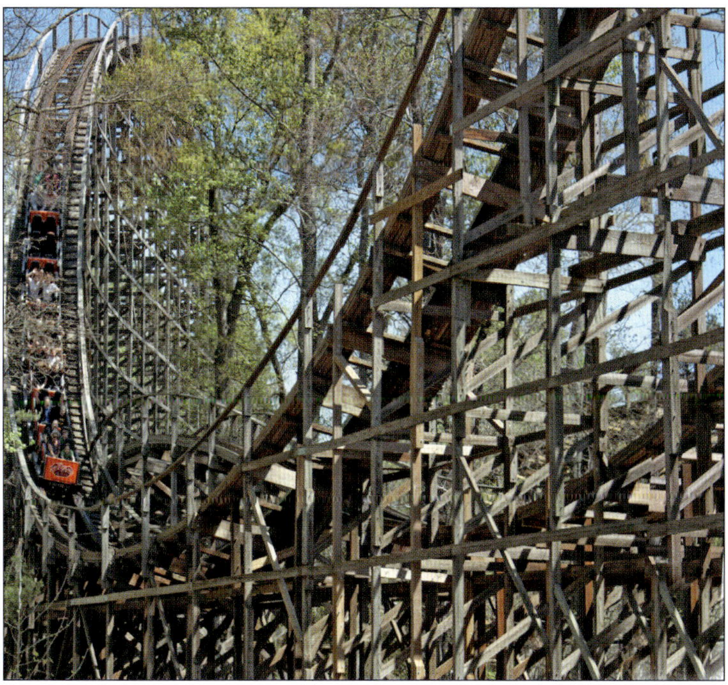

The coaster was built in the dense forests of Old Virginia. Night rides on this beast were especially exciting thanks to the lack of any illumination outside of the boarding station. Like Ohio's Wildcat before it, Grizzly spawned three other clones: Grizzly at California's Great America, Wilde Beast at Canada's Wonderland, and Bush Beast at Wonderland Sydney. Kings Dominion's excellent version is often voted to be the best.

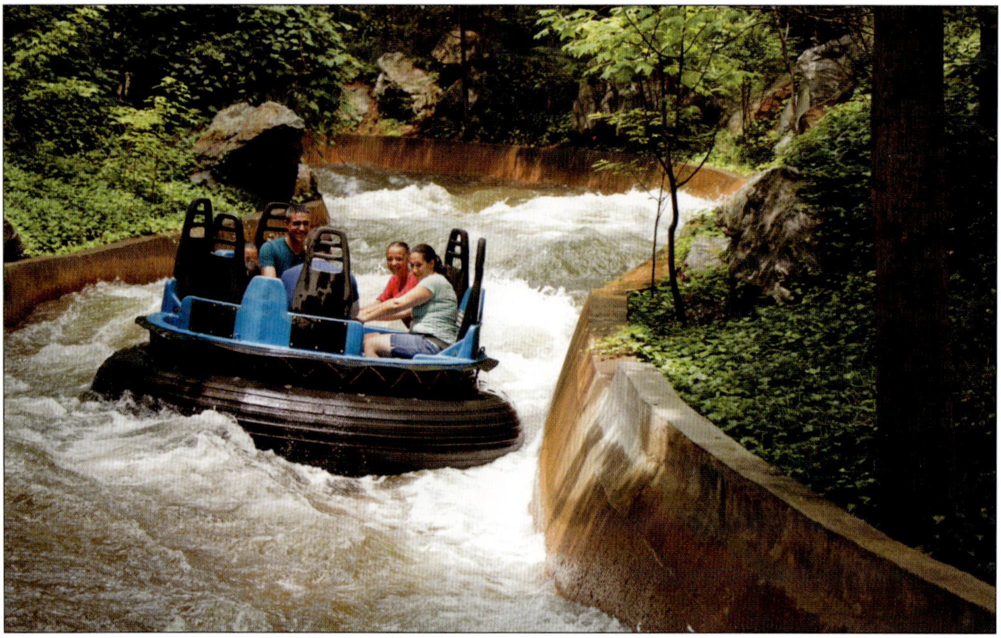

In 1983, Kings Dominion added White Water Canyon, another water adventure in the Old Virginia area near the Shenandoah Lumber Company log flume. The park's newest ride utilized a fleet of circular six-seat boats and an operating system supplied by Intamin. It followed a 1,500-foot-long unpredictable river channel through the woods that was filled with waterfalls, geysers, and other surprises.

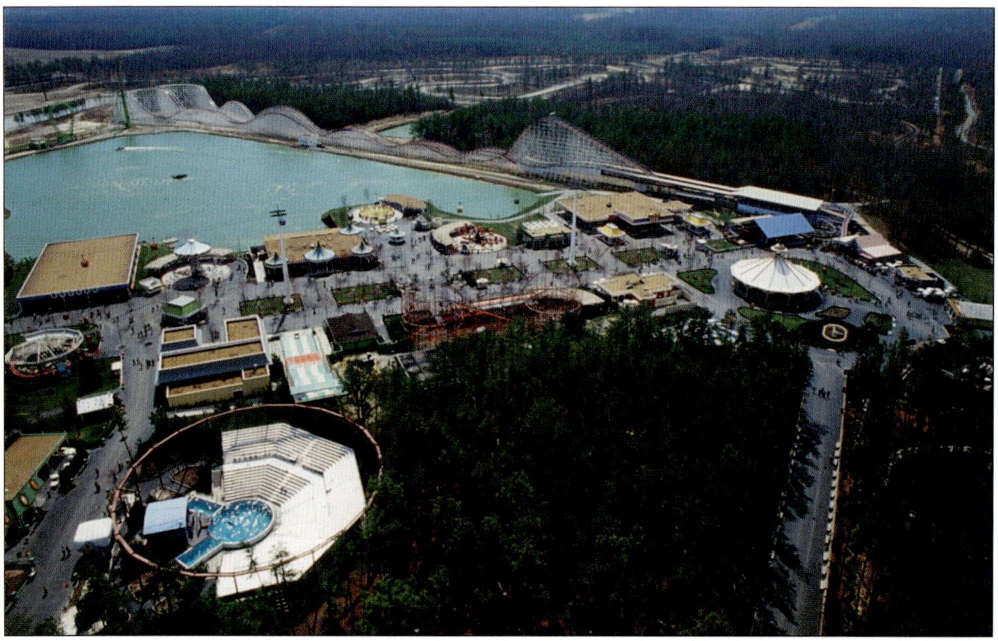

As compared to a similar construction view at the close of chapter one, this aerial image taken from the Eiffel Tower shows a bustling day on the Candy Apple Grove midway (formerly known as Coney Island). Unbeknownst to guests, this would be the last year under the direction of Taft Broadcasting.

Four

The KECO Years

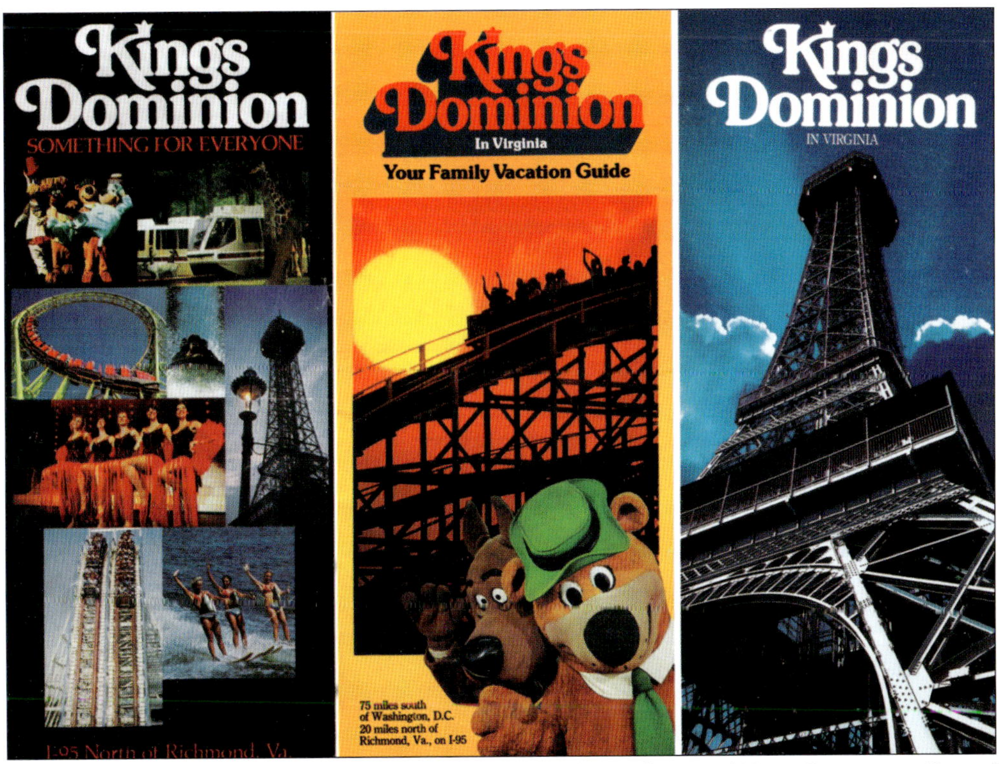

Brochures dating from 1978, 1981, and 1984 illustrate the evolution of Kings Dominion. One of the most significant changes in the park's history up until that point was under way for the 1984 season. In late 1983, a number of Taft Broadcasting's senior officials pooled their resources and purchased the theme park division of Taft for $167 million. This alliance would be known as Kings Entertainment Company (KECO).

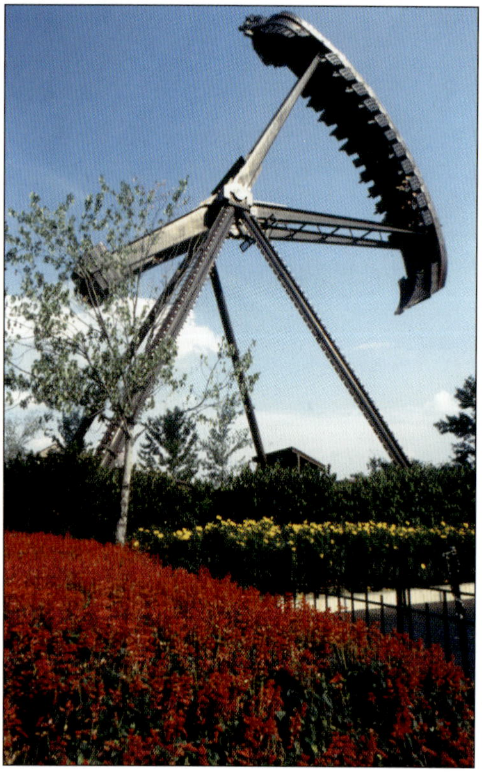

One of KECO's first additions was to purchase and install an Intamin Looping Starship ride on International Street in 1984. Sporting the appropriate name of Berserker, the new ride offered guests the sensation of being in a rocking galleon on the high seas. As an added bonus, the ship was able to complete a number of 360-degree rotations in either direction.

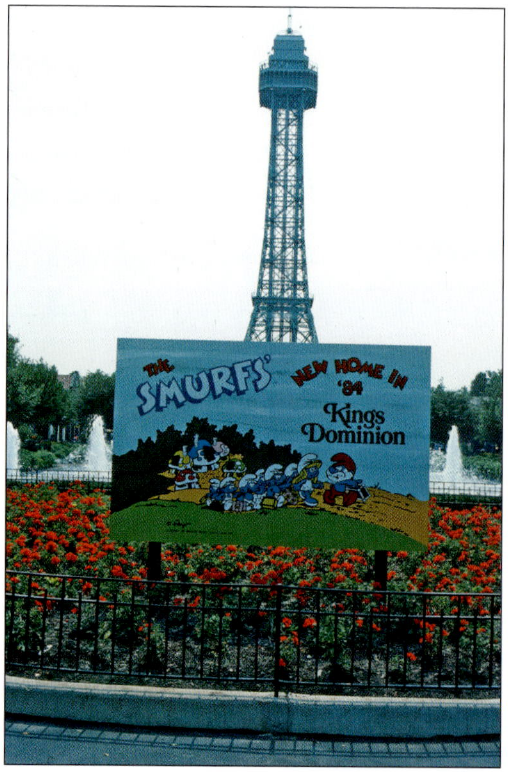

Another major development for Kings Dominion's 1984 season was the addition of the Smurfs, the Belgian comic and television franchise. Their presence was no more apparent than in the Lost World complex. The former Journey to the Land of Dooz mine train ride was renamed and re-themed as Smurf Mountain.

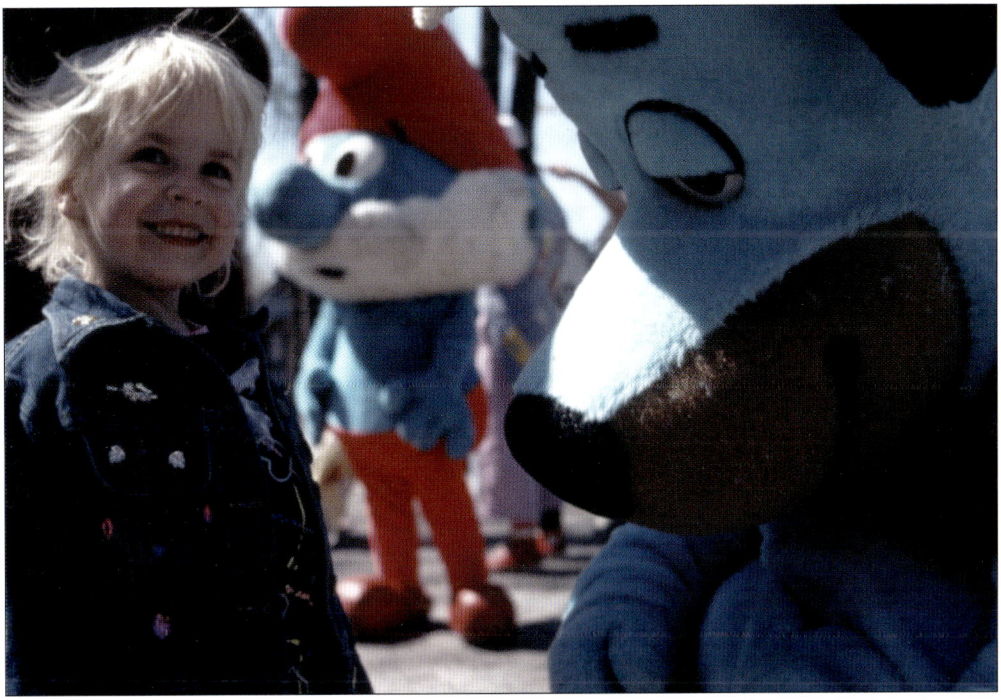

Not only were the Smurfs living in Smurf Mountain, but they could also be found in live shows as well as roving costumed characters. Here, Papa Smurf looks on as this little girl has her photograph taken with Huckleberry Hound, a Taft creation.

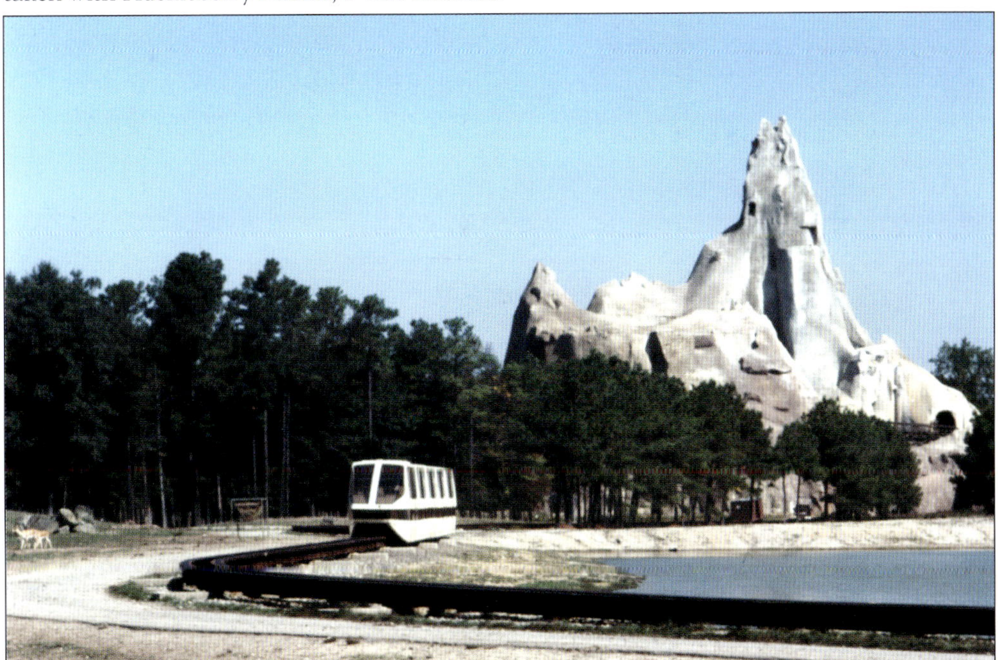

The Lost Mountain looms over the trees as the Wild Animal Safari Monorail leaves the park proper for an extended tour of the animal habitats. The excursion through the various animal areas took approximately 20 minutes.

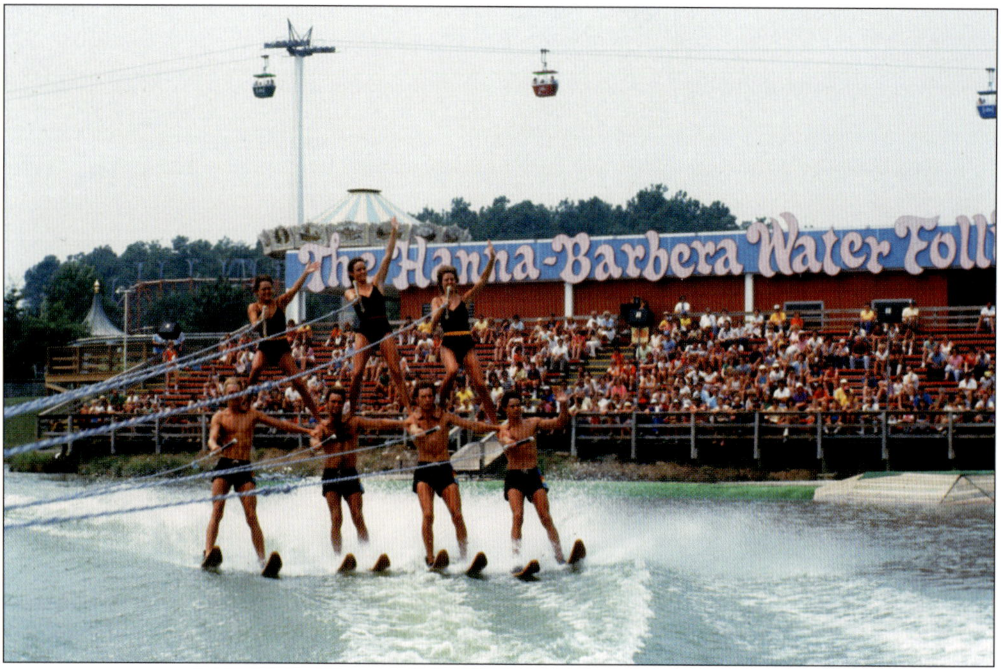

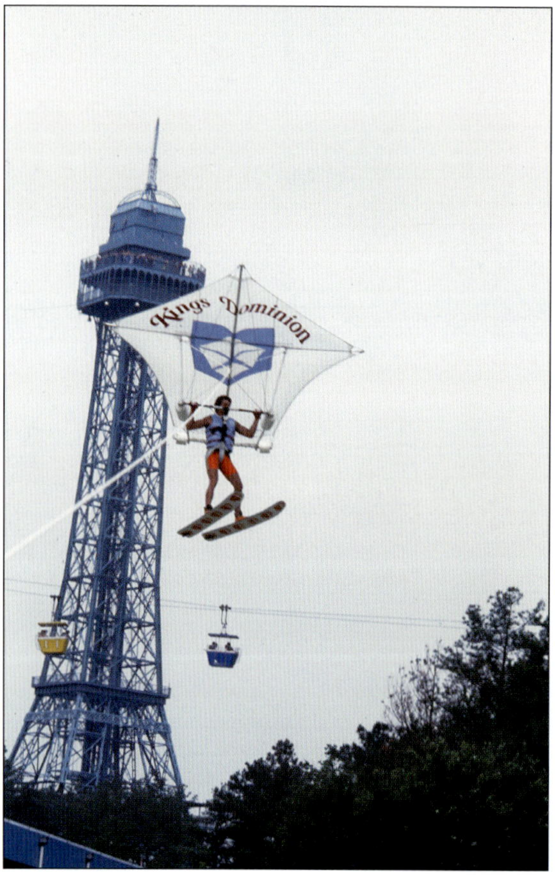

The Hanna-Barbera Water Follies was a 35-minute show that featured a talented team consisting of nine professional skiers who performed a variety of stunts, jumps, various formations, and other water-based acrobatics. Often, Hanna-Barbera costumed characters Jabber Jaw and Yogi Bear would join the show.

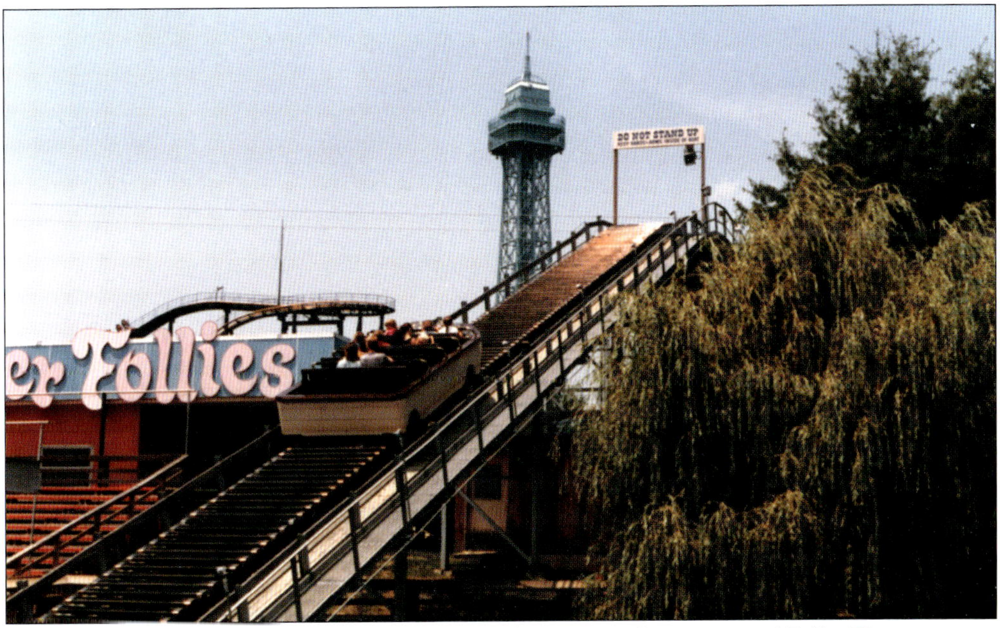

The 1985 season saw the introduction of yet another water ride—Diamond Falls. The attraction amounted to a modern version of Shoot the Chutes, a boat ride that was all the rage in the early 1900s. Supplied by Intamin at cost of $4 million, Diamond Falls featured 20-seat boats that were hauled to their highest point via chain lift; they then plunged down a 70-foot, pseudo-double dip into the splashdown.

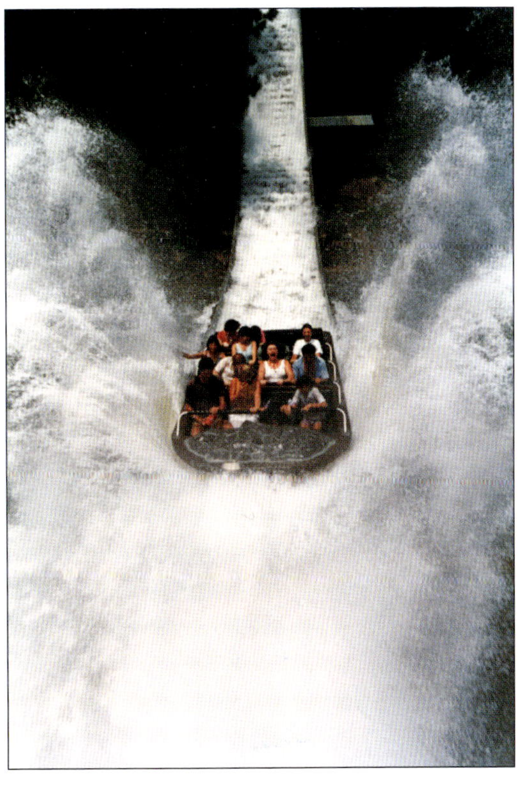

Diamond Falls' heavy boats generated a gigantic 50-foot wave that not only soaked riders, but it also drenched onlookers who happened to find themselves on a foot bridge situated near the base of the big drop. Once through the splashdown, the boats would float into an abandoned diamond mine where they came face to face with a dragon. From there, the boats made their way back into station.

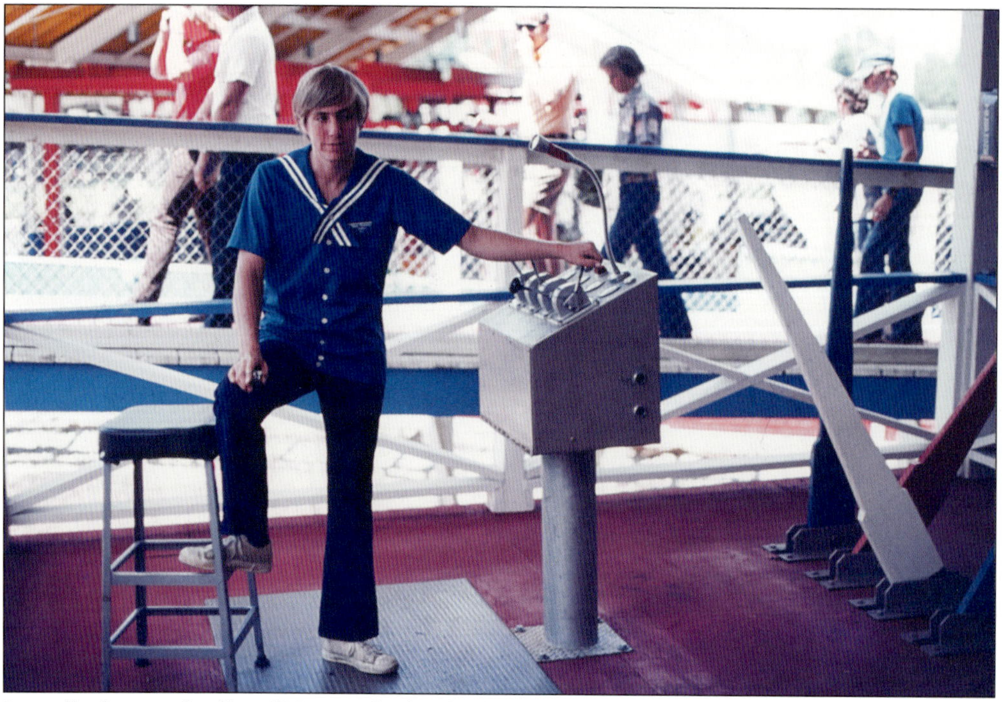

Literally thousands of local Virginia high school and college students spent time working at Kings Dominion during its first decade of operation. This image depicts a young man at the helm of one side of Rebel Yell. The control lever in his left hand is used to raise or lower the brakes that will either stop or release the two trains under his watch.

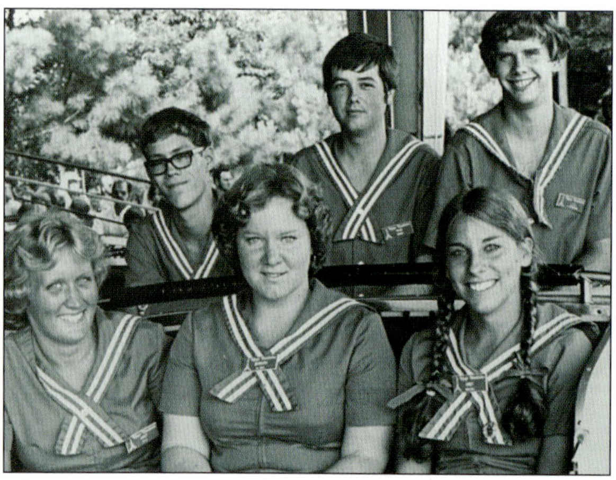

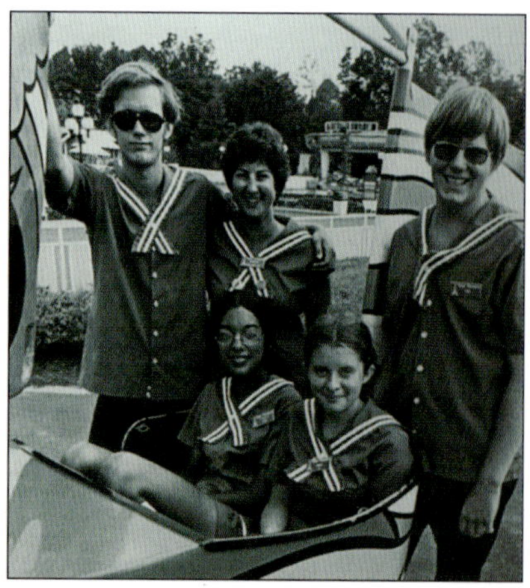

These two groups of rider operators take a moment to pose for their photographs, which will appear at the end of the season in the yearbooks the park assembled. The group on the left was assigned to the Vertigo (also known as Himalaya) in Candy Apple Grove while those at right were part of the team that took care of the Parrot Trooper (Flying Scooter) at its new location partially over the water on a platform near Safari Village.

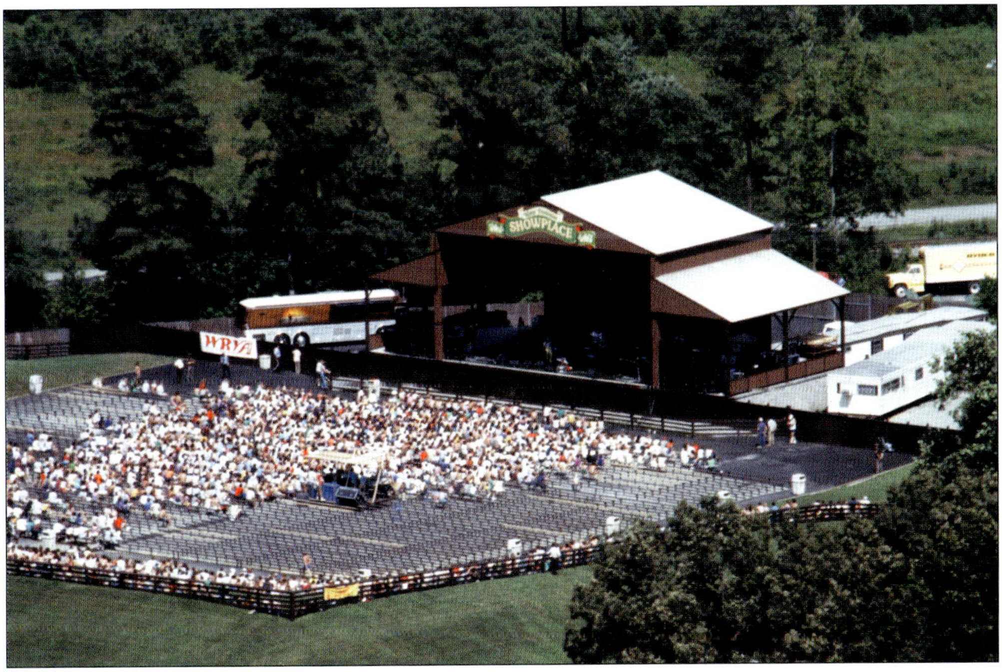

The Showplace was still packing them in after having opened to the public in 1982. This outdoor concert venue could accommodate up to 7,500 guests and significantly expanded Kings Dominion's live entertainment offerings by bringing in outside performers and various other acts.

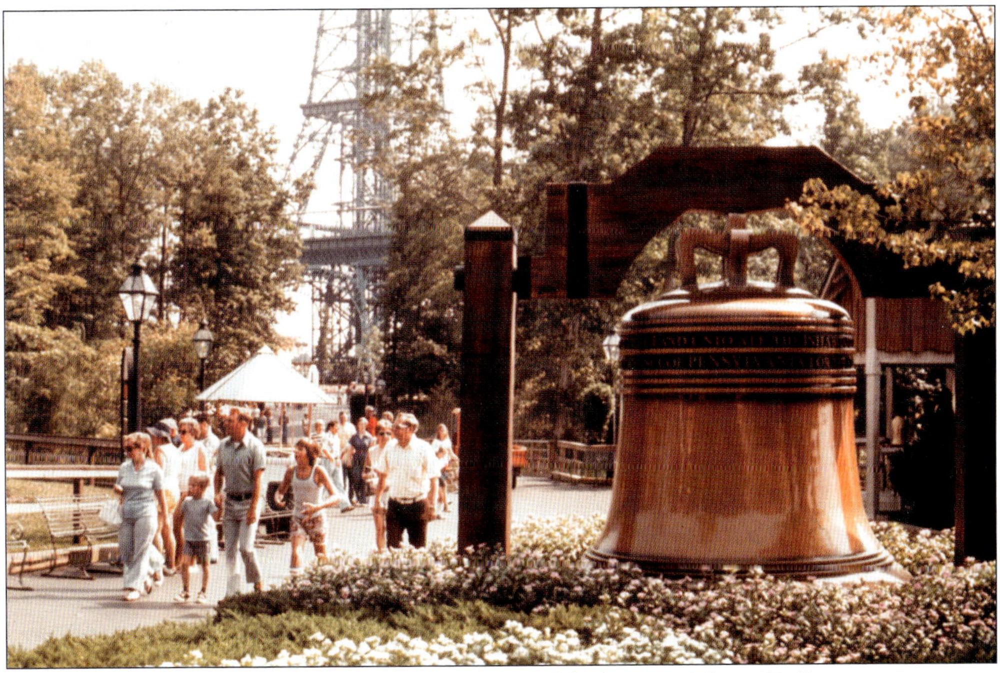

Located in Old Virginia, Kings Dominion's replica of the historic Liberty Bell sits on prominent display surrounded by colorful flower. The Liberty Bell was often used as a background in guest photographs.

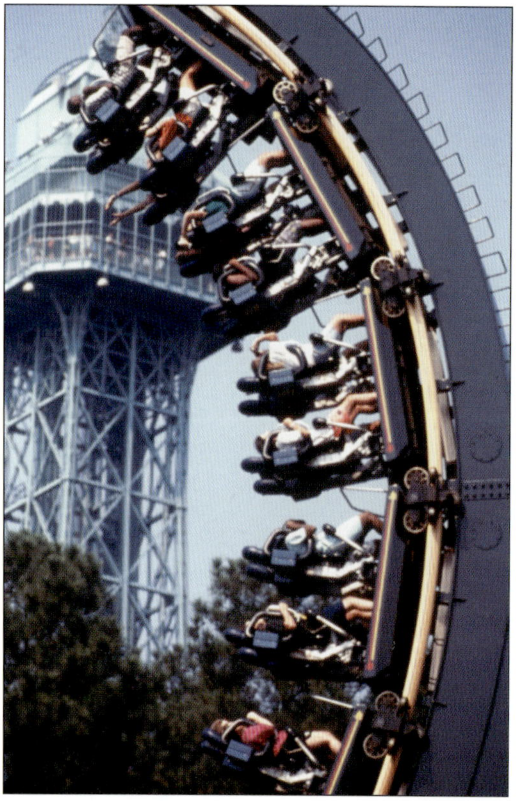

Kings Dominion's 1986 season was highlighted by the introduction of the park's next steel roller coaster, Shockwave. Manufactured by TOGO of Japan, it was the first stand-up coaster on the East Coast. Unfortunately, the addition of Shockwave necessitated in the removal of the Galaxi, as the new coaster was built on the same plot of land in Candy Apple Grove. The Galaxi was relocated to the Pavilion at Myrtle Beach, South Carolina.

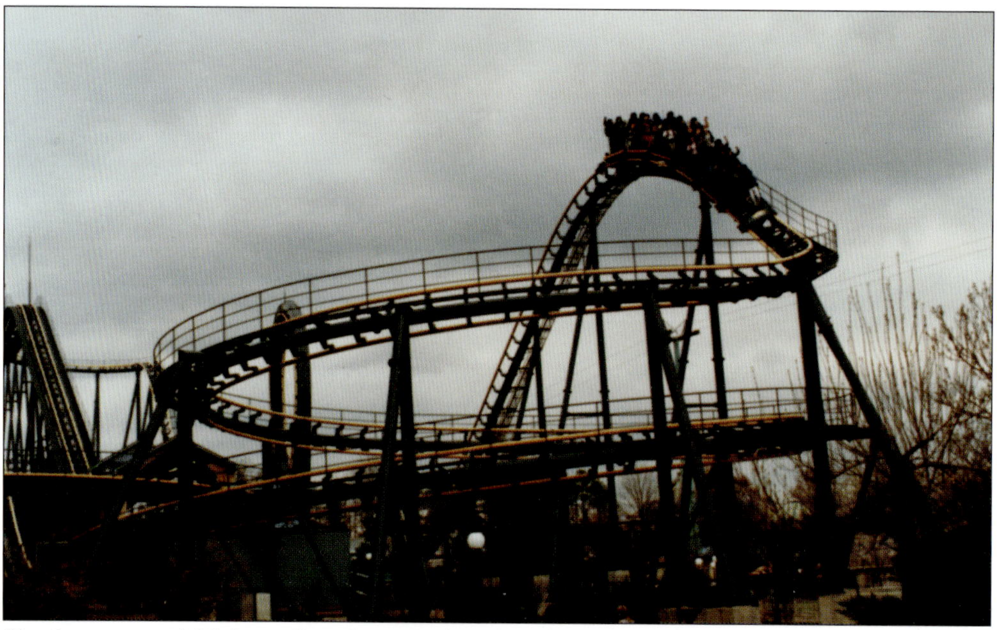

Shockwave stood 95 feet tall with an 84-foot first drop that led directly into a vertical loop. Guests were then treated to a high-G downward spiral, several speed bumps, and two other turns that comprised the 2,231-foot-long course. Two other significant removals in 1986 included both Wacky Wheels and the beloved King Kobra.

The 1987 season brought Racing Rivers, a precursor to a full-blown water park that would follow several years later. A collaboration between KECO and New Wave Rides, Racing Rivers was the place to be to get wet and cool off at Kings Dominion, all while wearing regular street clothes. Racing Rivers featured three different waterslides: Torpedo, Riptide, and Splashdown.

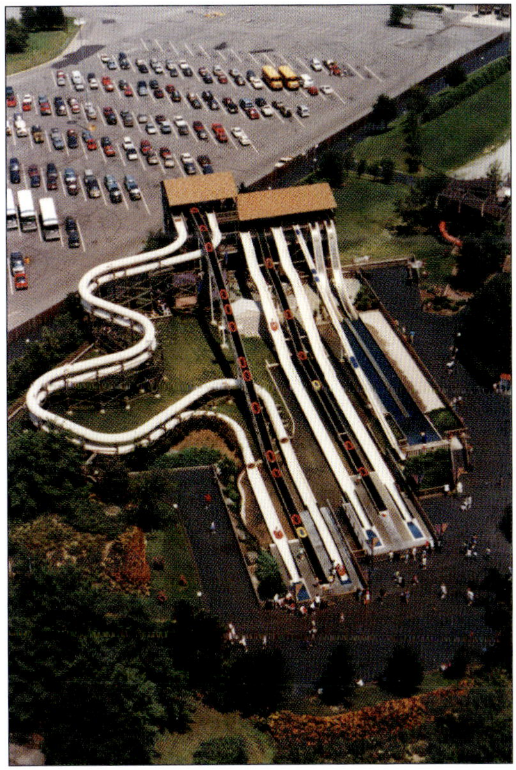

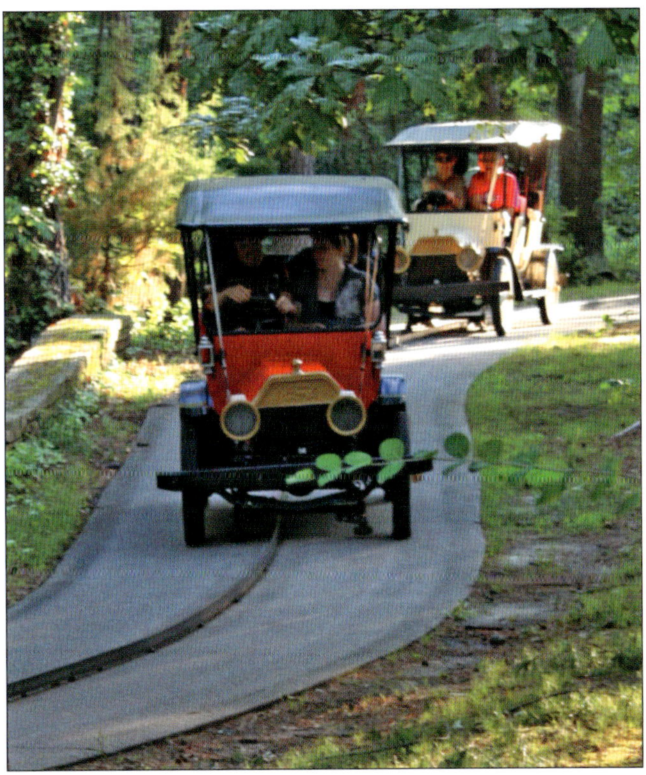

Another way to cool off was to take a leisurely drive on the Blue Ridge Tollway. Another Arrow Development creation, these gasoline-powered, Model T–styled cars offer guests a quiet getaway as they meander through the dense trees of the Old Virginia forest.

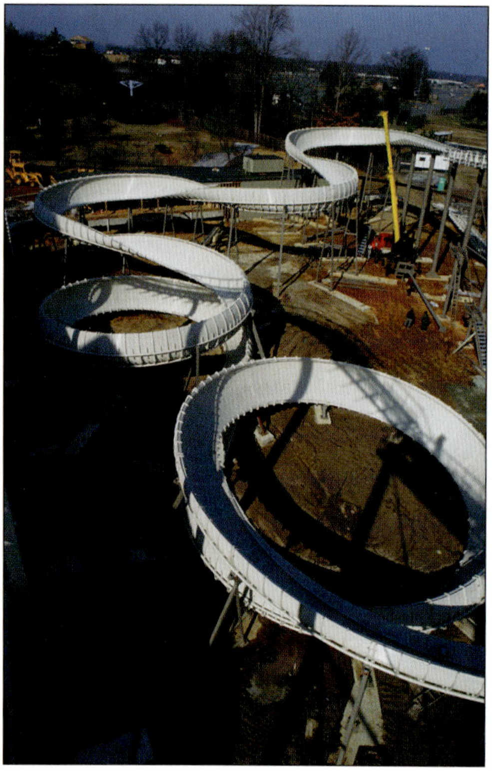

The 1988 season saw the arrival of a most unique new attraction—Avalanche. The new roller coaster would feature seven-car trains free-wheeling inside of a concave trough. Pictured here during construction is the ride's trough, which was comprised of a number of individual steel tubes combined to form a running surface for the trains' polyurethane wheels.

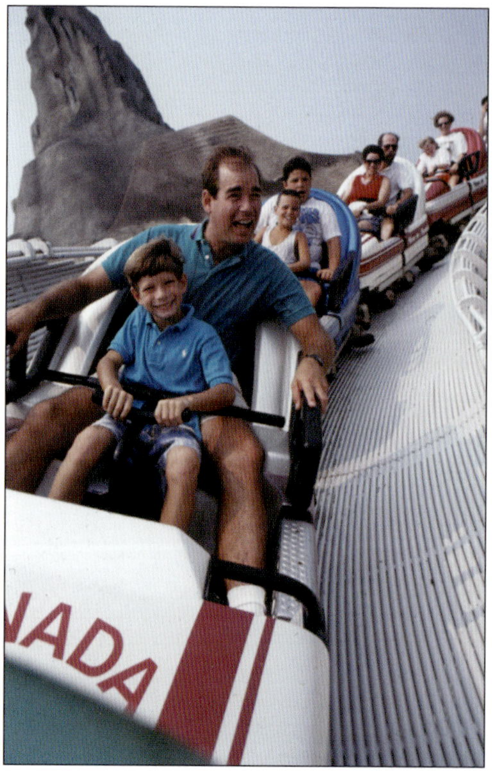

Manufactured by Germany's Mack Rides, Avalanche would be the only such ride in North America. The Avalanche is actually a steel re-creation of an early-20th-century wooden coaster, the Flying Turns. As with the old Flying Turns, this image shows how Avalanche guests ride tandem-style (one between the other's legs) for a total of 28 passengers per train.

The Sky Pilot touched down at Kings Dominion in 1989. From 90 feet up in the air, riders had control of the cockpit and could determine their own flight pattern with joysticks, enabling them to take a smooth flight or extend their ride vehicle arms out for a 360-degree spin. The Sky Pilot was supplied by Intamin.

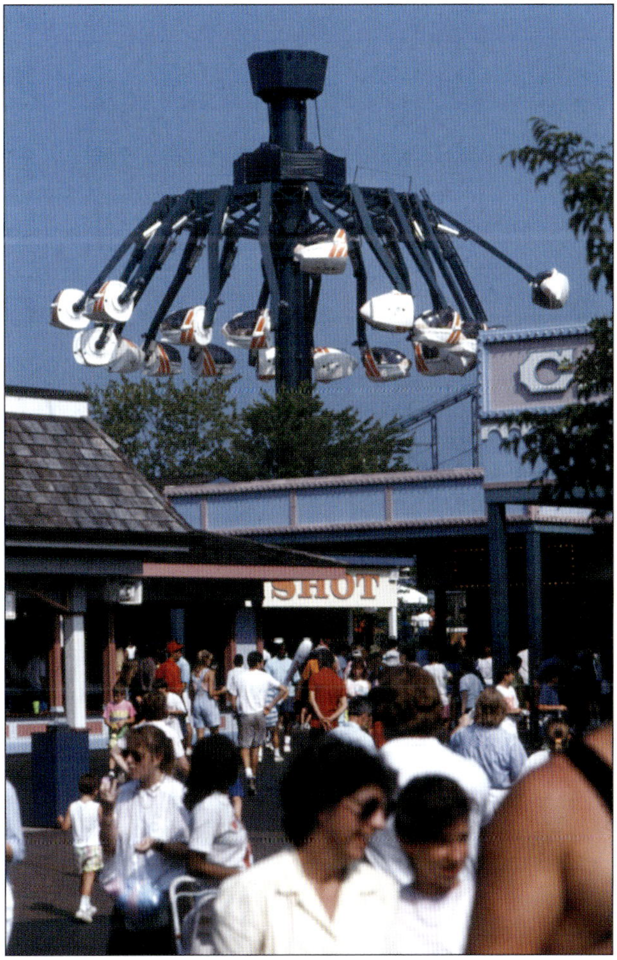

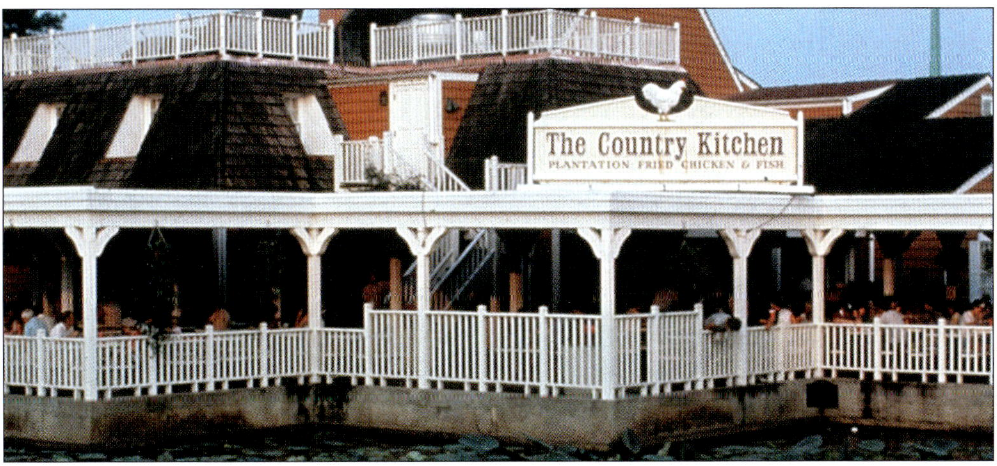

Spending a full day in a theme park can work up hearty appetites. Kings Dominion offered a vast number of dining options, including both grab-and-go kiosks as well as a number of counter service restaurants. The Country Kitchen (pictured here) was one of the most popular. This old-fashioned southern counter service restaurant specialized in "plantation fried chicken and fish."

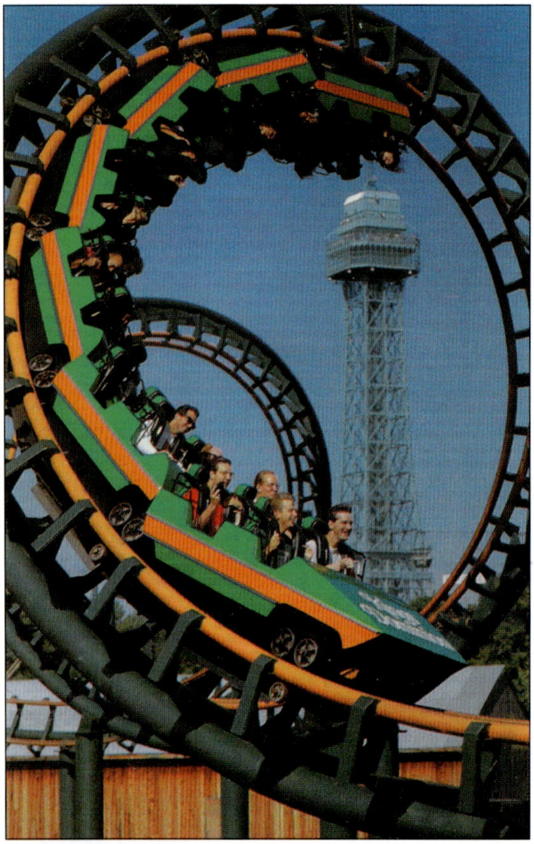

In 1991, Kings Dominion and Arrow Dynamics (formerly Arrow Development) created Anaconda, a steel-looping roller coaster constructed over a section of Lake Charles. The ride's station and 128-foot-tall lift hill were built on land formerly occupied by King Kobra. Anaconda featured 2,700 feet of track, most of which was built above Lake Charles.

With Rebel Yell in the background, this image shows Anaconda's curving first drop that plunged toward the surface of Lake Charles and then into an underwater concrete tunnel. This aspect brought the total first drop length to a surprising 144 feet. The new coaster took riders on a 50-mile-per-hour journey that offered a total of four inversions (vertical loop, sidewinder, and two corkscrews).

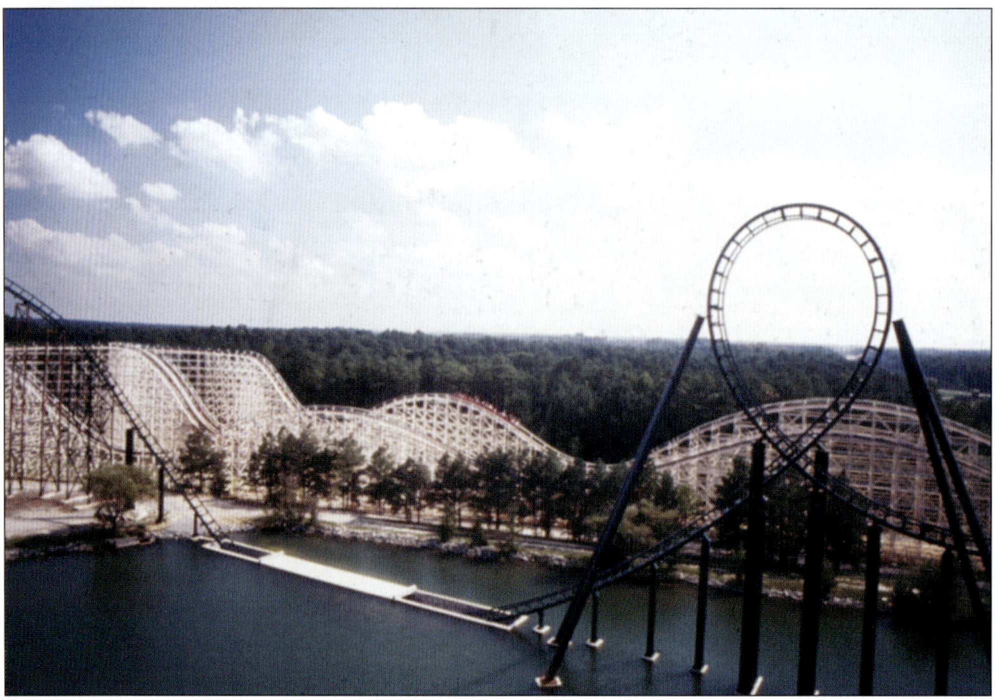

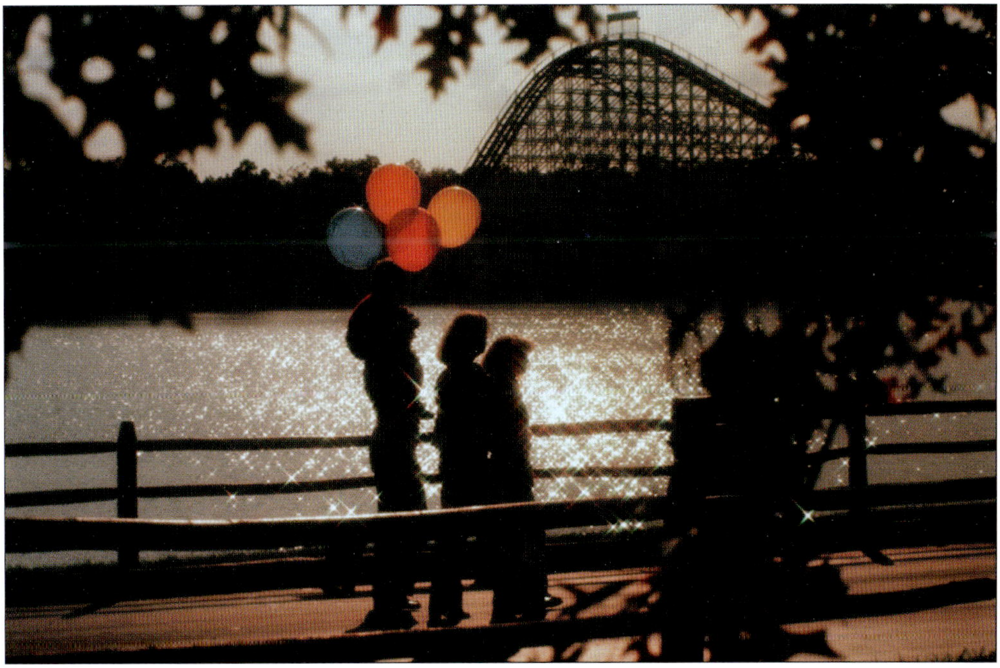

For many, theme parks are all about the rides—the faster the better. But sometimes, it is just as nice to take a break, as this family is doing, with a stroll along the glittering surface of Lake Charles. Rebel Yell's lift hill and first drop are visible across the water.

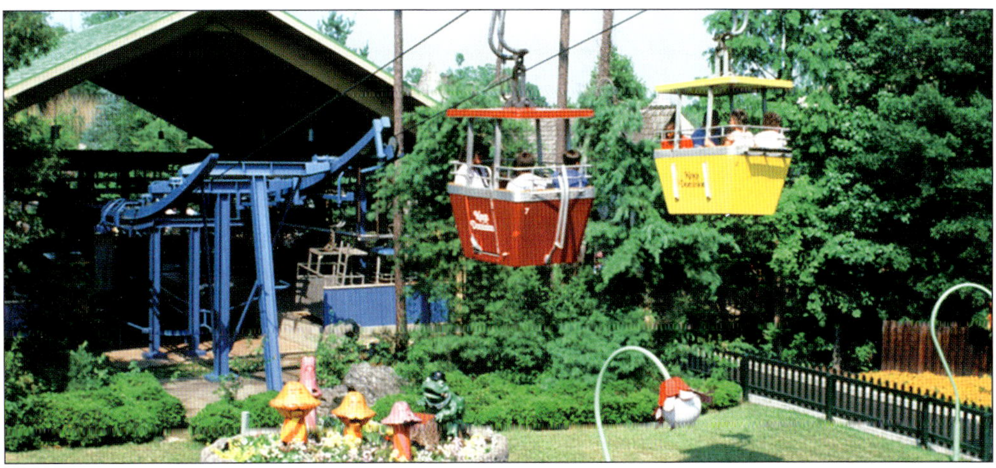

In the same vein, the Sky Ride was always the perfect way to have seat and just watch the world glide by below. This view shows the drive side of the attraction. The blue steel rails lift the gondolas off the cable as they are unloaded with arriving passengers and filled with those departing this station, which is near the entrance to Safari Village. The Singing Mushrooms are in performance mode.

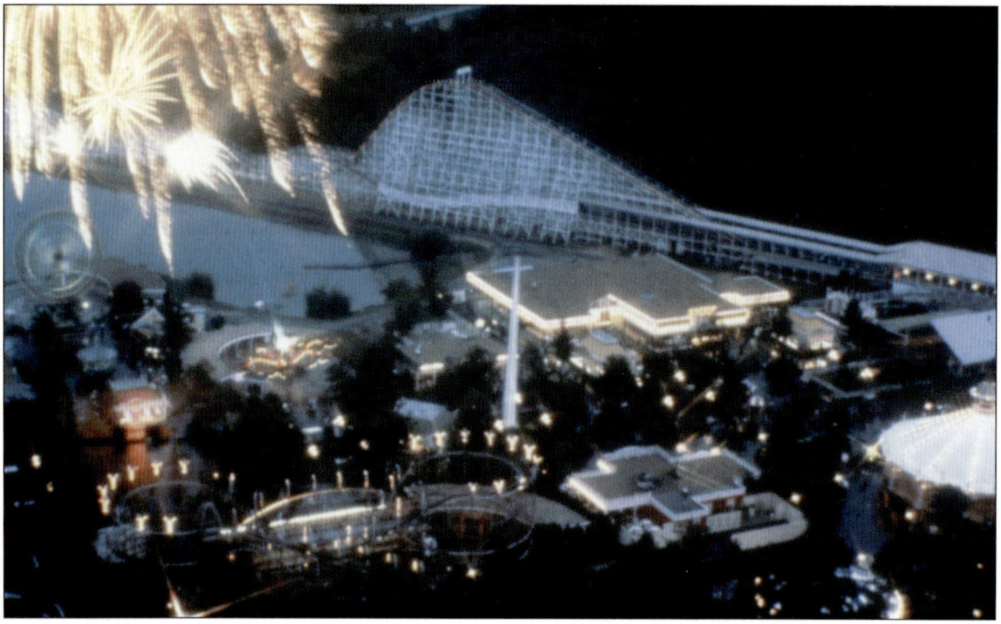

Candy Apple Grove's rides and attractions twinkle and glow like miniatures as evening descends and the fireworks begin. Parts of this scene would soon be a thing of past. In 1992, two-thirds of Lake Charles would be filled for the addition of Hurricane Reef, a six-acre water park. Not only would the lake be reduced in size, but Apple Turnover (seen in motion at the water's edge) would be removed.

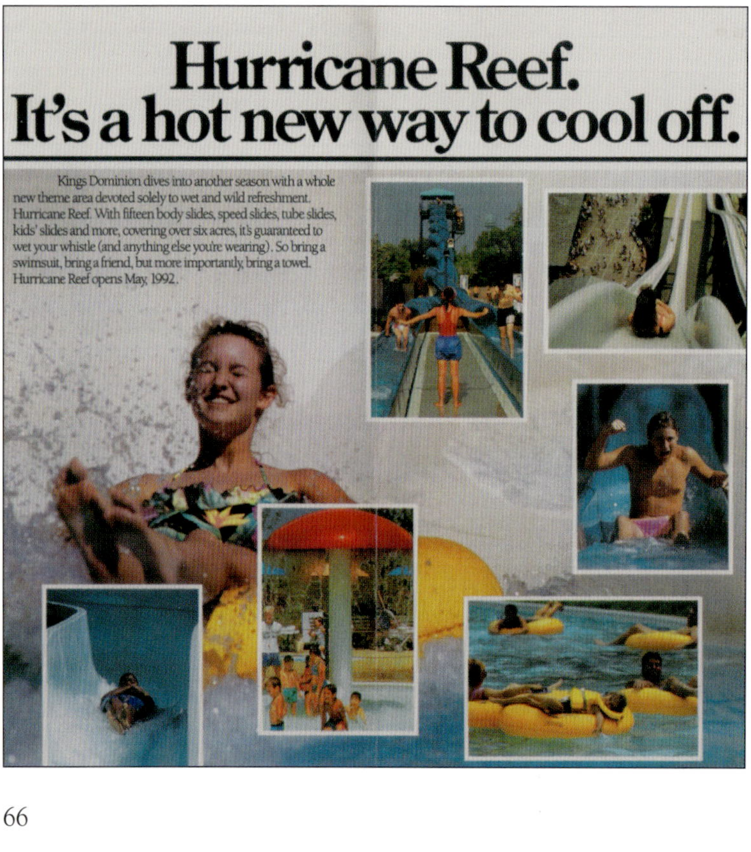

Hurricane Reef.
It's a hot new way to cool off.

Kings Dominion dives into another season with a whole new theme area devoted solely to wet and wild refreshment. Hurricane Reef. With fifteen body slides, speed slides, tube slides, kids' slides and more, covering over six acres, it's guaranteed to wet your whistle (and anything else you're wearing). So bring a swimsuit, bring a friend, but more importantly, bring a towel. Hurricane Reef opens May, 1992.

Constructed in 1992 just off the Candy Apple Grove midway, the $4.5 million Hurricane Reef would feature 15 waterslides of various heights, lengths, and configurations. In addition, the water park would offer an endless river through which guests floated on tubes as well as an area dubbed Splash Island, which sported pint-sized waterslides geared toward families with young children. This 1992 brochure offers a glimpse of all the new water park offered.

Five

Paramount Parks

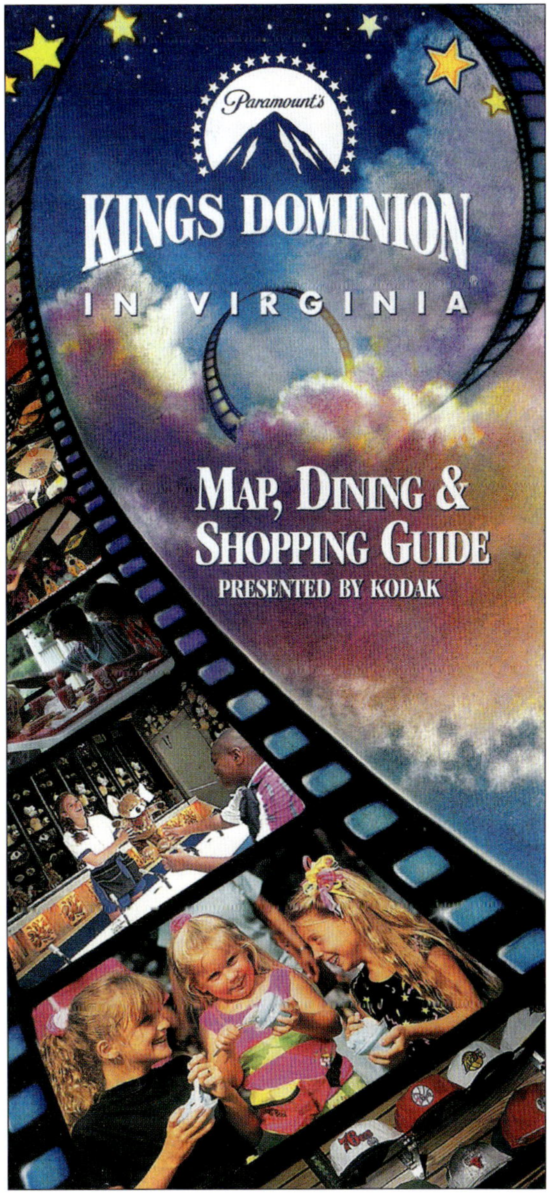

In 1993, Paramount Communications, Inc., purchased Kings Dominion and its other properties from KECO. The park's name was changed to Paramount's Kings Dominion, while the sister parks had "Paramount" attached to their own names. While this was good news to a degree, it also meant many facets of the former park would be phased out rather quickly. Victims of that first season included Lion County Safari and Smurf Mountain.

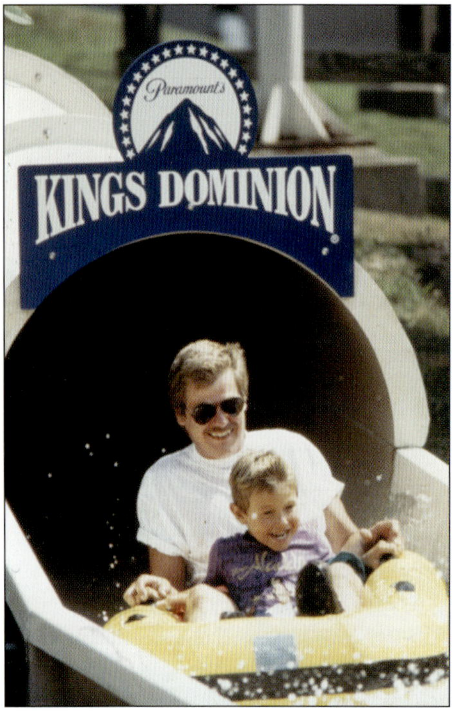

Upon the arrival of Paramount, the brand's signage was attached to many of Kings Dominion's existing rides and attractions. The park's name along with the familiar studio logo—with its conical mountain peak and 22 stars—is pictured here above the exit of the Torpedo, an enclosed tube slide at the Racing Rivers complex.

The first of the original Paramount-themed attractions was Days of Thunder, a motion simulator opened in 1993 in the Action Theater. Themed around Paramount's 1990 Tom Cruise film *Days of Thunder*, the new ride combined a 3-D film along with seats on motion-based platforms meant to offer guests an approximation of what it felt like to be behind the wheel of a speeding race car.

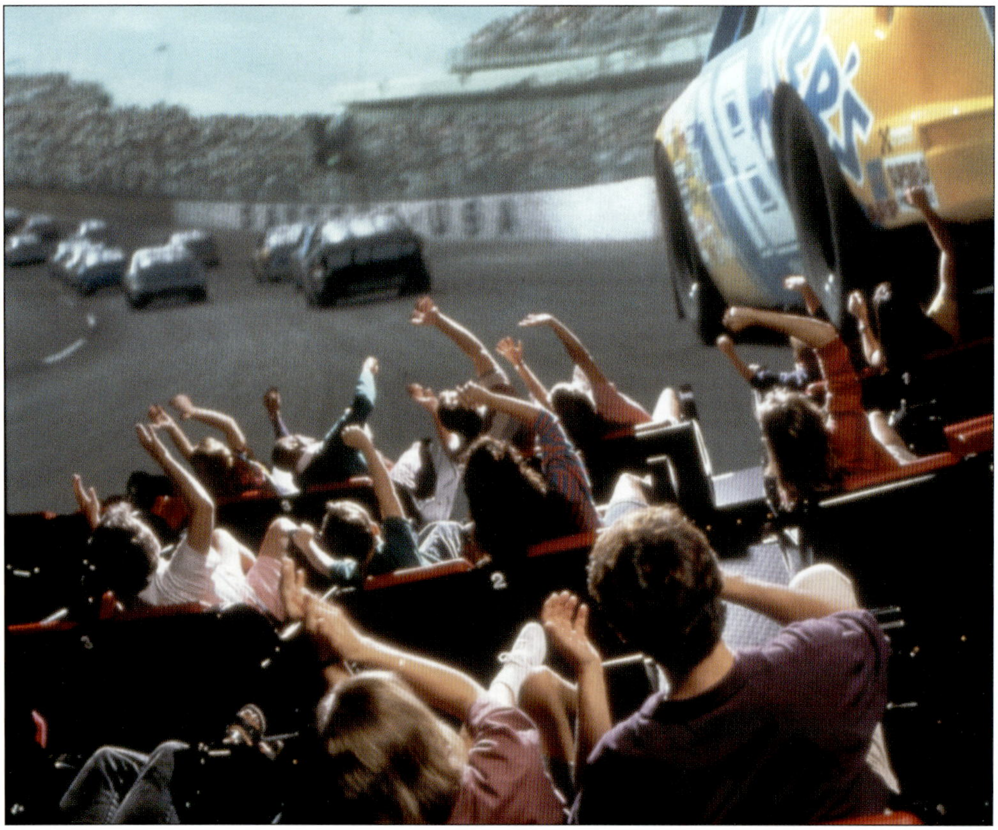

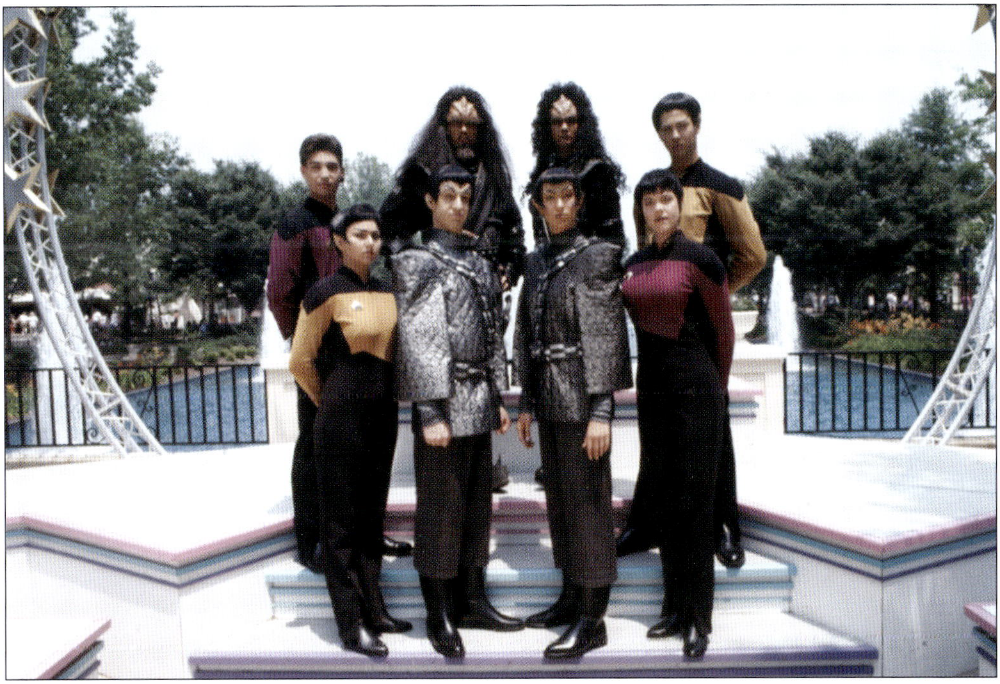

Paramount quickly made its presence known in virtually every aspect of Kings Dominion. The *Star Trek* film and television franchise (above) was well represented by employees acting as both Starfleet personnel as well as Romulans and Klingons, pictured here at the front of International Street. The image on the right was captured during a publicity shoot that most likely had a few kids surprised to see Klingons aboard a speeding Scooby-Doo train.

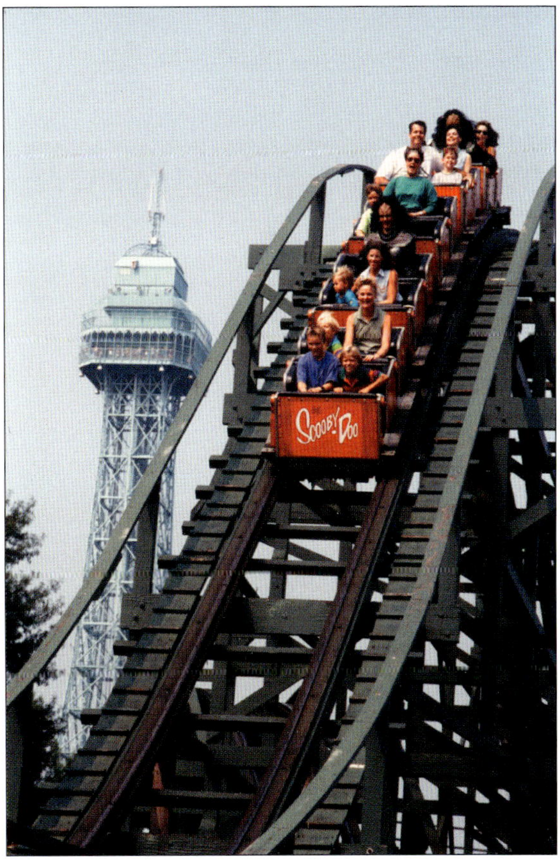

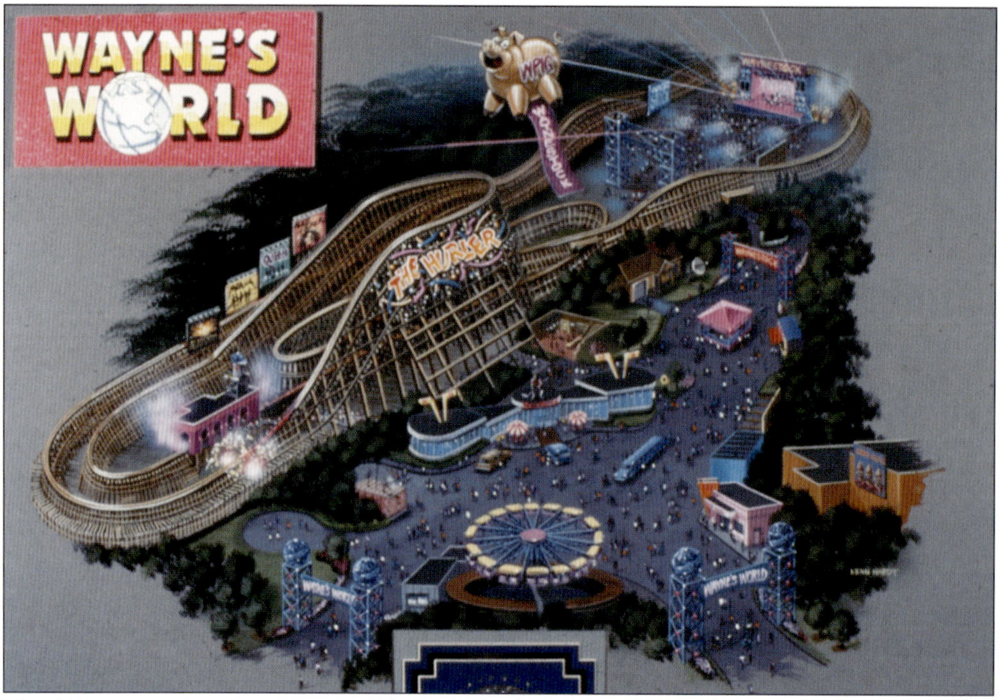

The 1994 season found a new area of the park developed—Wayne's World. Based on the *Saturday Night Live* skit as well as a 1992 Paramount film, the section featured the Rock Shop and a Stan Mikita's restaurant. Interestingly, this promotional rendering shows an Enterprise ride, which may indicate this was also used to illustrate Carowinds' version of Wayne's World. Kings Dominion relocated the Flying Scooter here and renamed it Scream Weaver.

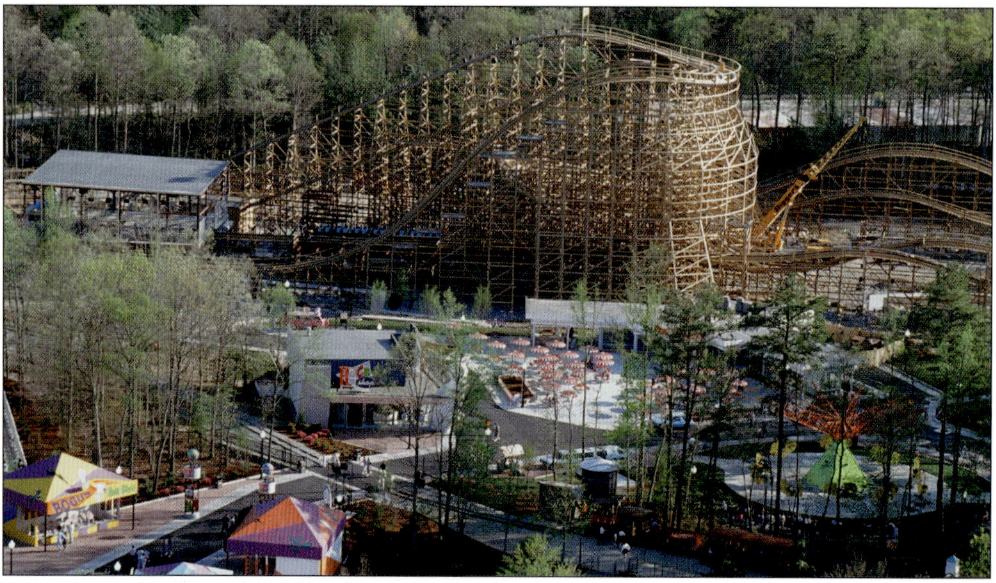

Wayne's World was anchored by the park's fourth wooden roller coaster, the Hurler. Shown here under construction in spring 1994, the Hurler stood 83 feet tall and featured 3,157 feet of track. An identical version opened the same year at Carowinds. The Hurler trains, painted robin's egg blue, were inspired by the 1976 AMC Pacer used in the film.

Nickelodeon Splat City was added to the park in 1995. The area offered a number of attractions inspired by several popular Nickelodeon television shows, including *Double Dare*, which involved activities where people would get wet. Pictured here are volunteers being subjected to the Nickelodeon "treatment." That same season, the Showplace was expanded, updated, and rededicated as the Kingswood Amphitheatre.

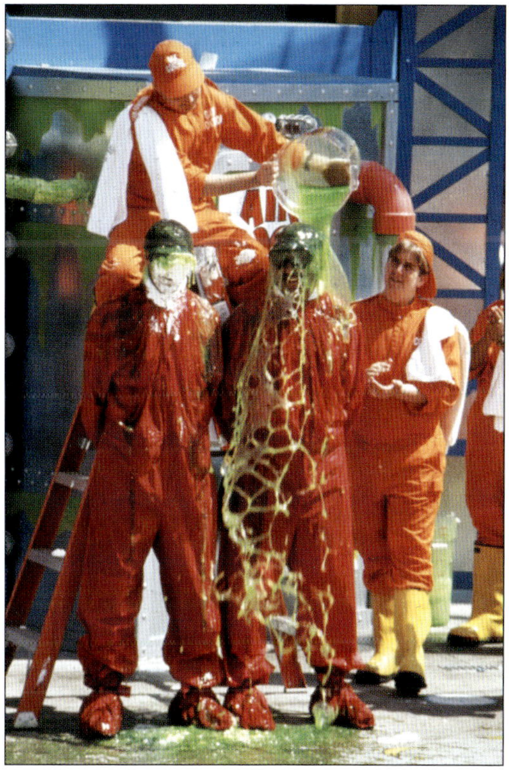

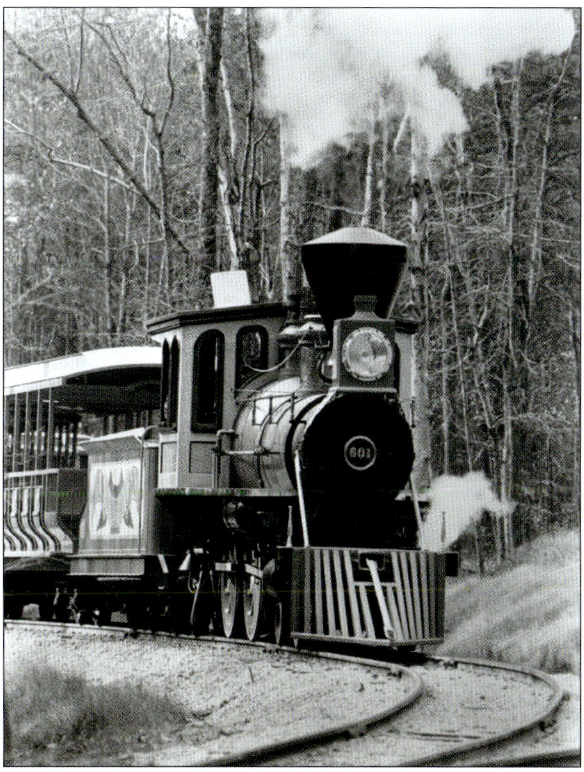

Though Paramount's influence was beneficial in that it brought expensive new attractions, there was a feeling that much of the park's original charm as well as its early rides were slowly being discarded. Even the original lands were not immune, with Candy Apple Grove becoming the Grove and Safari Village being renamed Congo. That same year saw the removal of the Haunted River, Time Shaft, and Sky Ride. Another victim of changing attitudes was the much-loved Old Dominion Line. This black-and-white image captures the train on one of its final runs at Kings Dominion. It too would soon fade into memory.

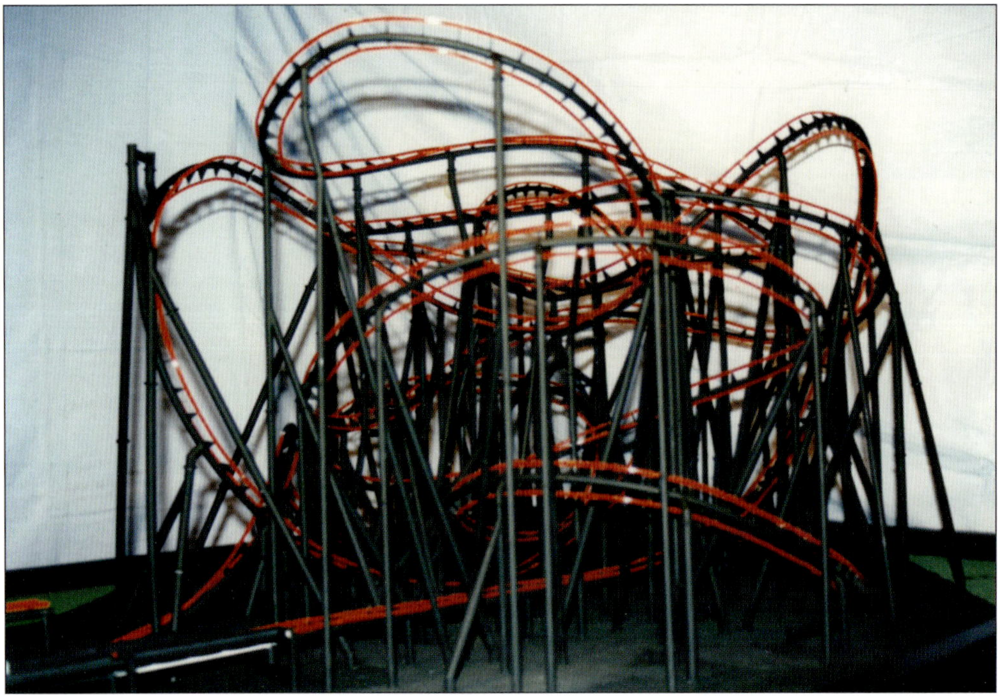

In 1996, one of Kings Dominion's most expensive and revolutionary rides to date made its debut—Outer Limits: Flight of Fear. Based on the *Outer Limits* television show, it and its twin at sister park Kings Island were the first coasters to utilize linear induction motor (LIM) to propel trains from 0 to 54 miles per hour in less than four seconds. This model illustrates the coaster's compact layout.

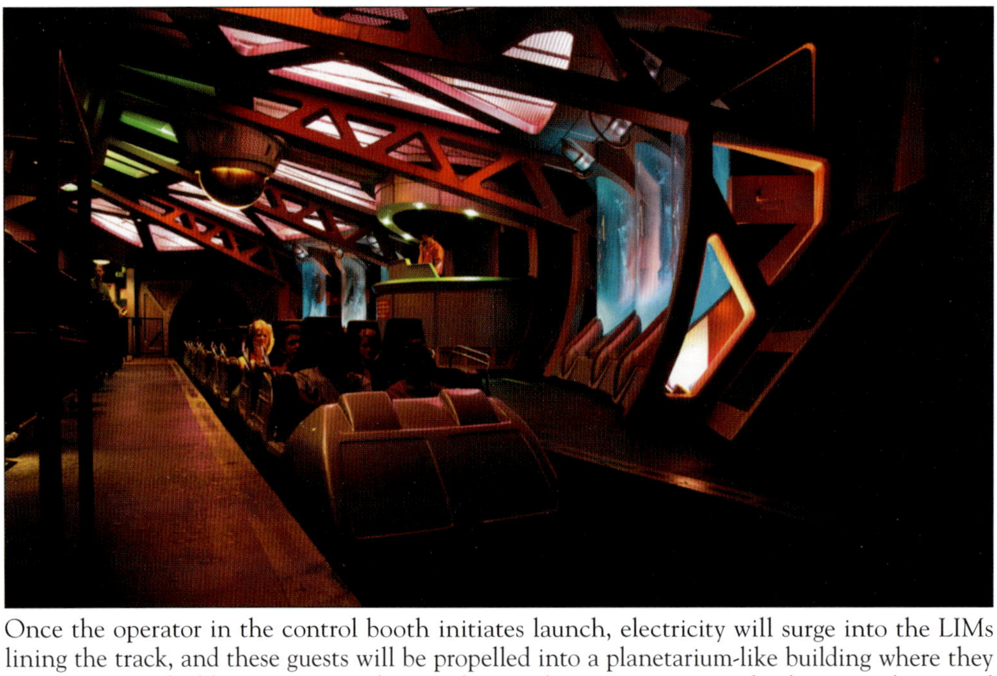

Once the operator in the control booth initiates launch, electricity will surge into the LIMs lining the track, and these guests will be propelled into a planetarium-like building where they negotiate a total of four inversions along with a confusing concoction of tight turns, drops, and other maneuvers in darkness.

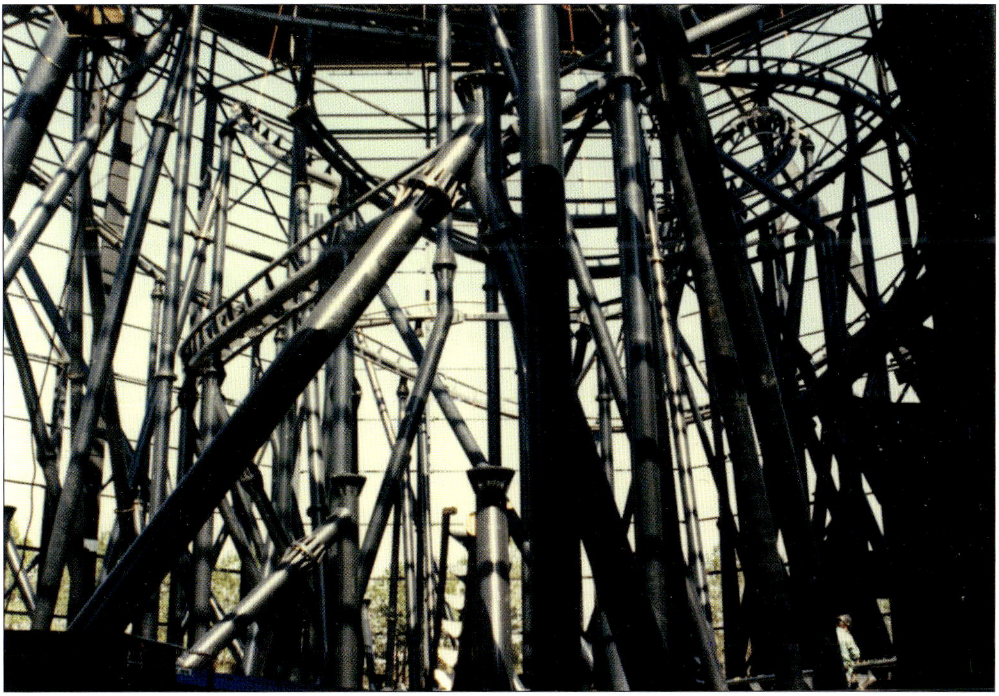

The coaster was designed by Germany's Werner Stengel and built by Premier Rides of Maryland. These two images were taken during construction before the walls of the main show building were attached. The accuracy in the design and execution of this coaster required a phenomenal degree of precision. Both Outer Limits: Flight of Fear installations won a number of amusement industry accolades.

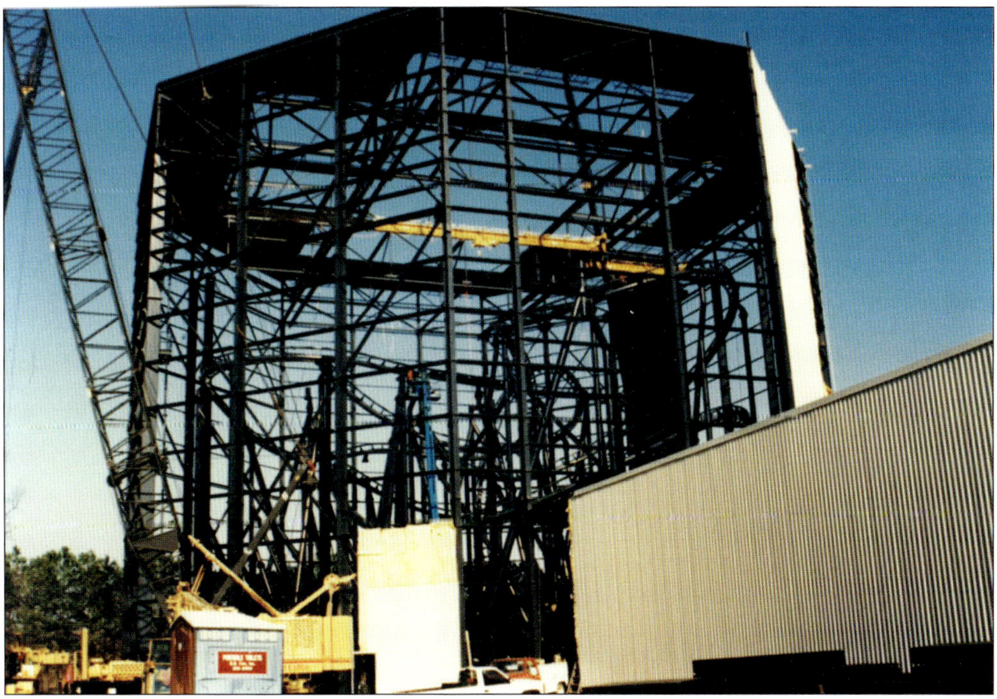

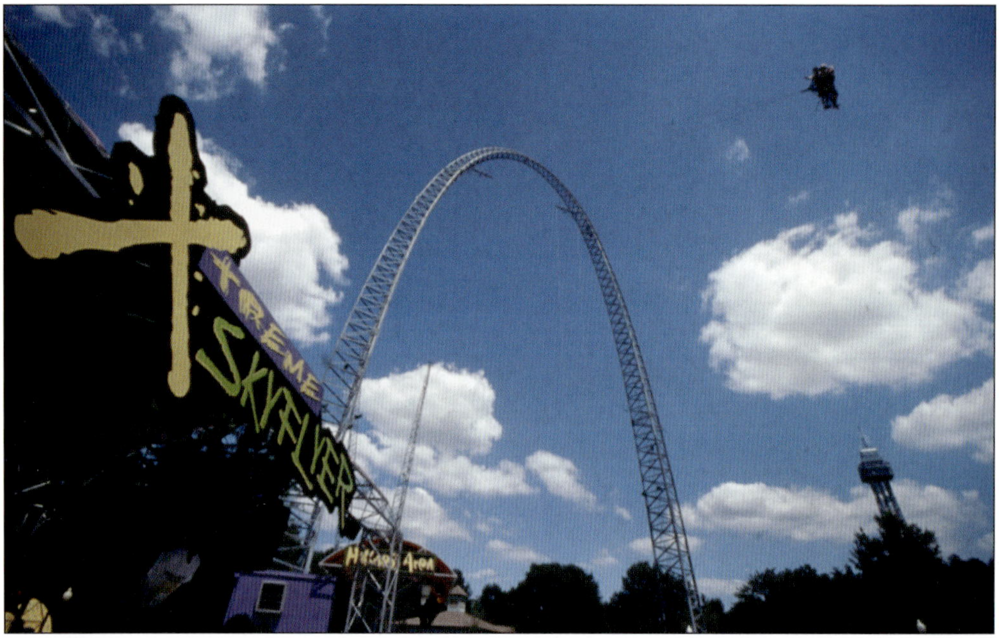

Xtreme Sky Flyer opened near the Wayne's World area in 1996. Supplied by Skycoaster®, Inc., the attraction offered guests the thrill of hang gliding and sky diving. One to three fliers would be harnessed and attached to cables suspended from an arch composed of galvanized steel. A motorized winch raised the fliers backwards to the height of a 15-story building. The fliers then pulled a ripcord, which released them.

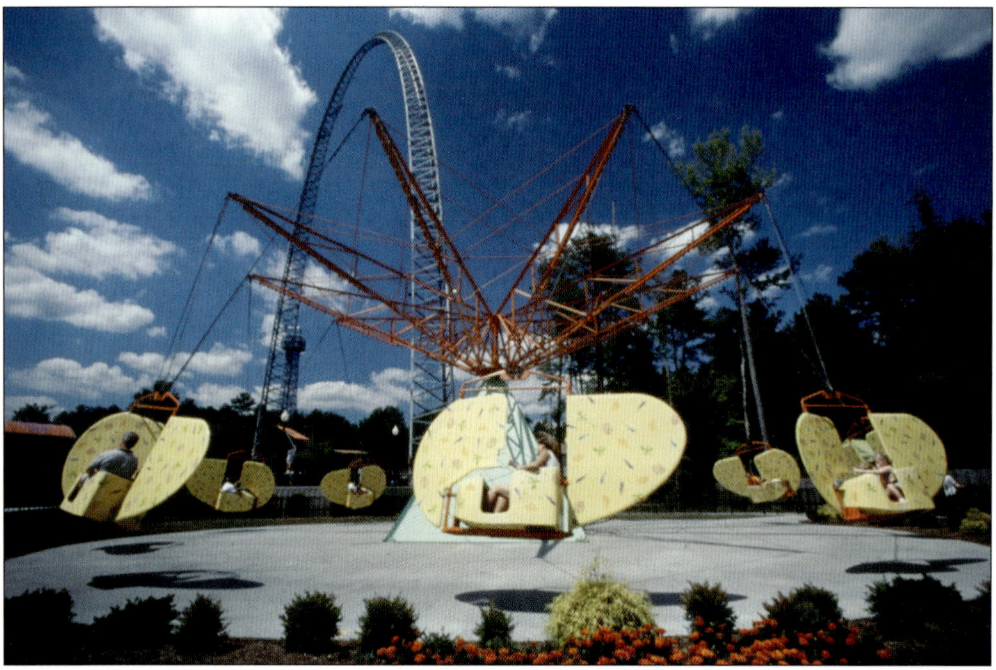

With the steel support arch of the Xtreme Sky Flyer looming above, the park's venerable Flying Scooter (formerly known as Parrot Trooper) gets a makeover and relocation to Wayne's World as the Scream Weaver.

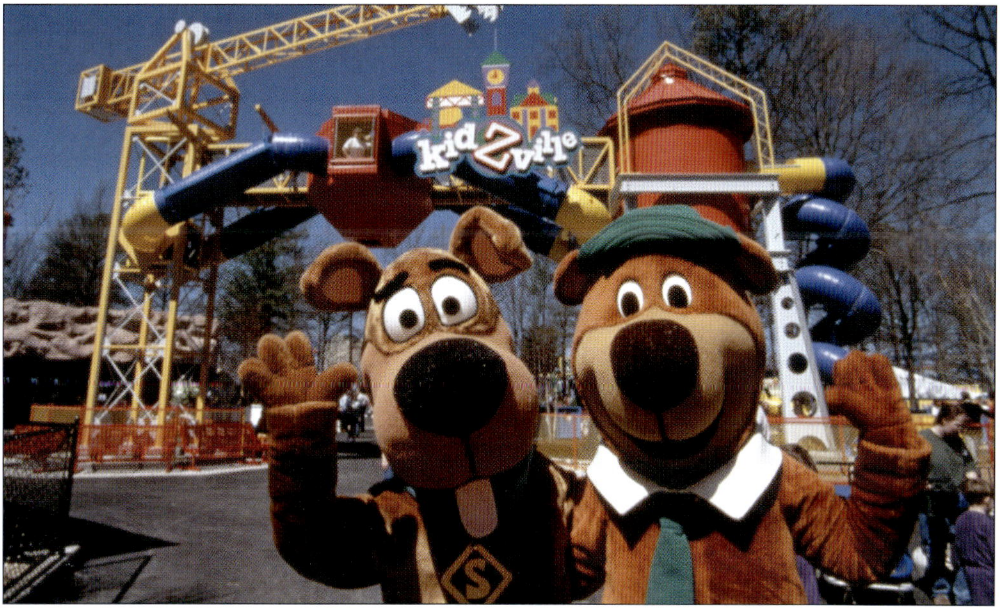

Debuting in 1997, KidZville was a re-theming of the former Hanna-Barbera section. Along with the addition of the Taxi Jam junior steel roller coaster, Kidz Construction Company replaced Scooby's Playpark while Yogi's Cave morphed into the Treasure Cave. However, the Hanna-Barbera brand would survive, with a number of rides retaining their original cartoon themes.

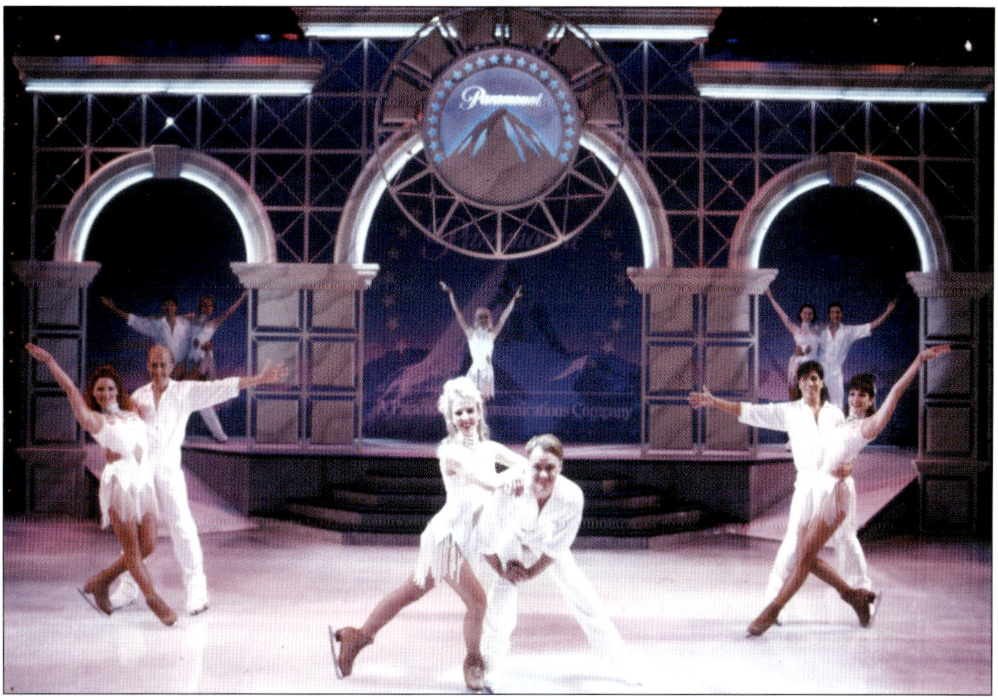

Paramount on Ice was one of the park's most ambitious and entertaining productions during the Paramount era. Held in the Paramount Theater (formerly the Mason Dixon Theater), the show featured an amazingly talented ground of skaters sporting lavish costumes and sets along with an original soundtrack that recalled the Golden Age of Hollywood.

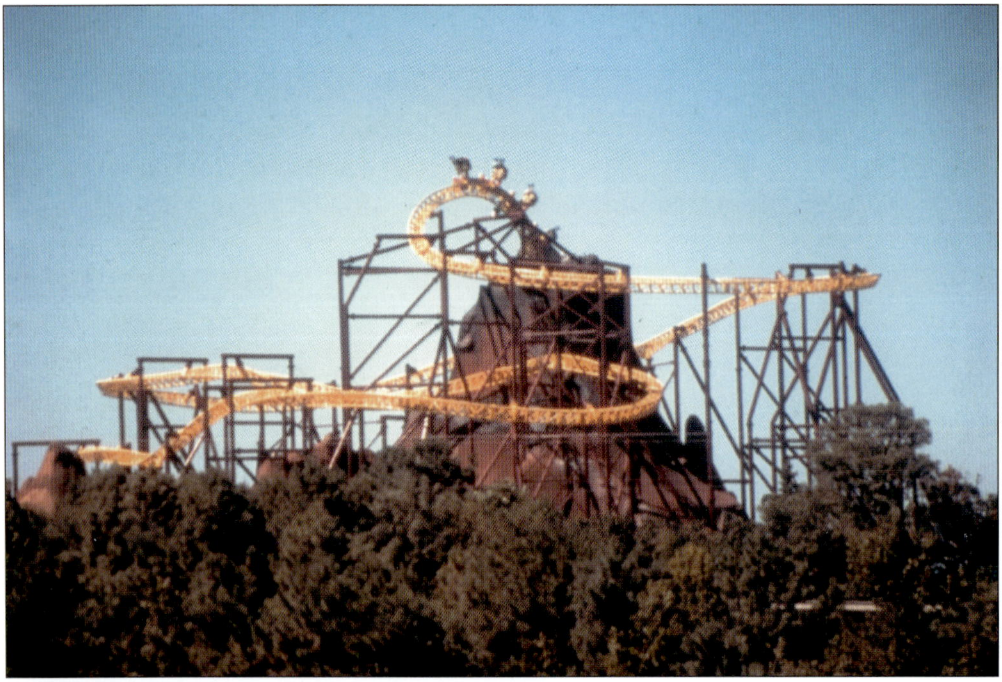

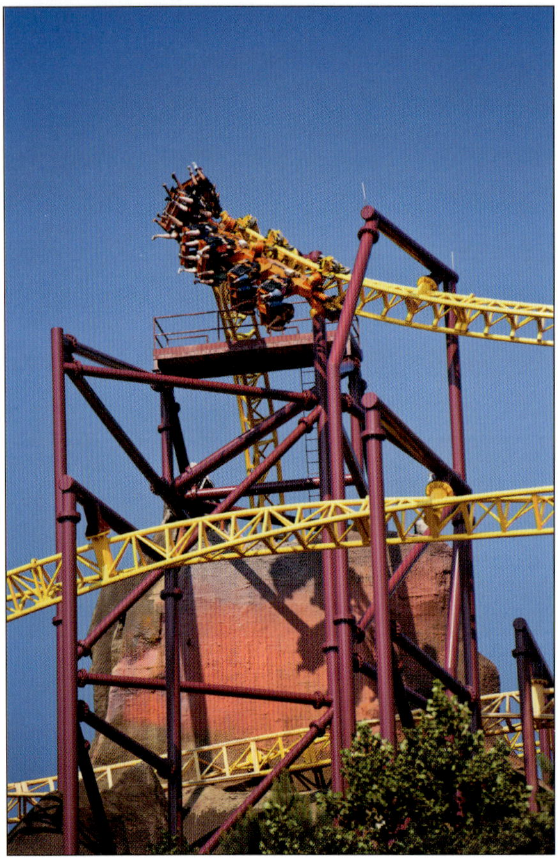

In 1998, the Lost World mountain complex (shuttered since fall 1995) would finally be repurposed. Paramount wanted a Volcano-themed steel roller coaster that used an LIM launch. Intamin was selected to design the ride. Using an inverted coaster system that featured ride vehicles rigidly suspended from an overhead track, it would be the first such full-circuit coaster to utilize LIM launch technology.

This image captures the train 155 feet above the ground blasting out of the Volcano lava tube as it begins its first inversion, a rollover. The remainder of the 2,757-foot-long layout that winds down and around the mountain features three heartline rolls, named due to the fact that the train rotates around the axis of the rider's heart instead of the coaster's seats. The ride concludes with a dramatic 80-foot swooping dive back into the mountain and into the braking area and station.

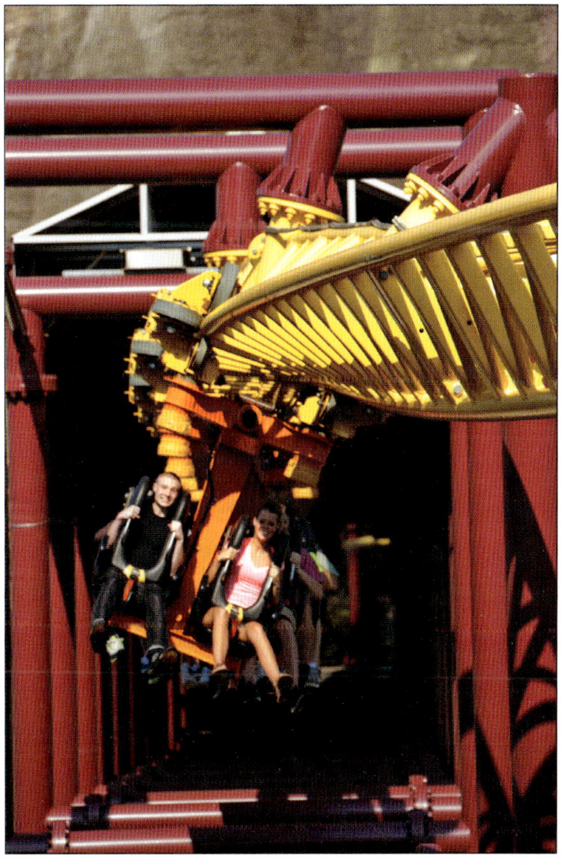

These two rare shots of Volcano—taken in the off-limits area—portray a train exiting the mountain at 70 miles per hour thanks to the first LIM launch. A sharp left 200-degree curve leads the train to a second set of powerful LIMs that accelerate and propel it back into the mountain and into an abrupt 90-degree vertical ascent that culminates in the rollover element at the top.

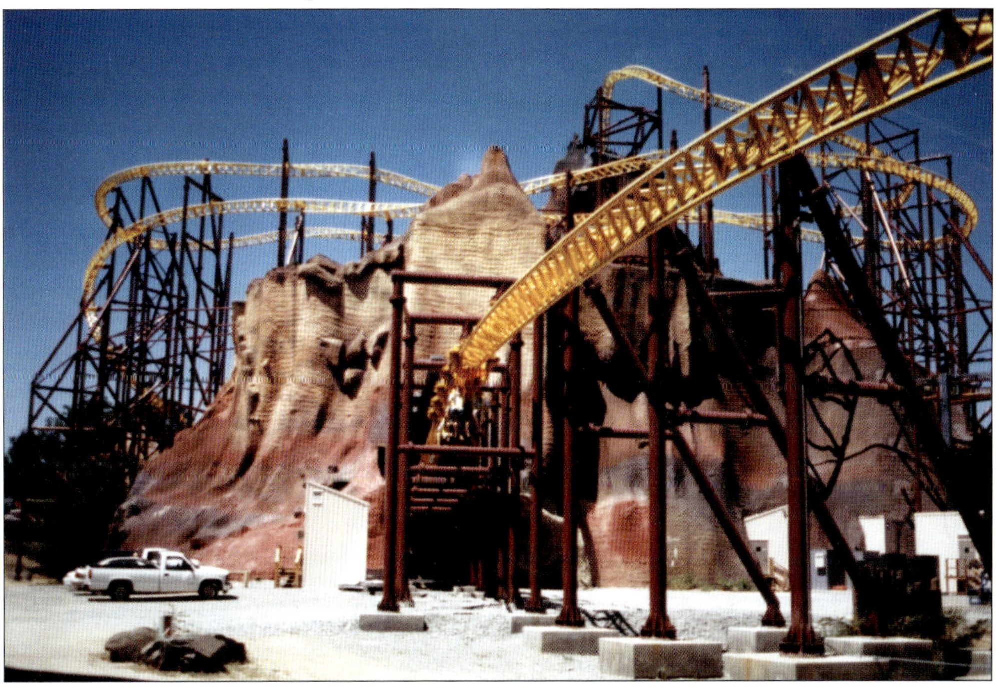

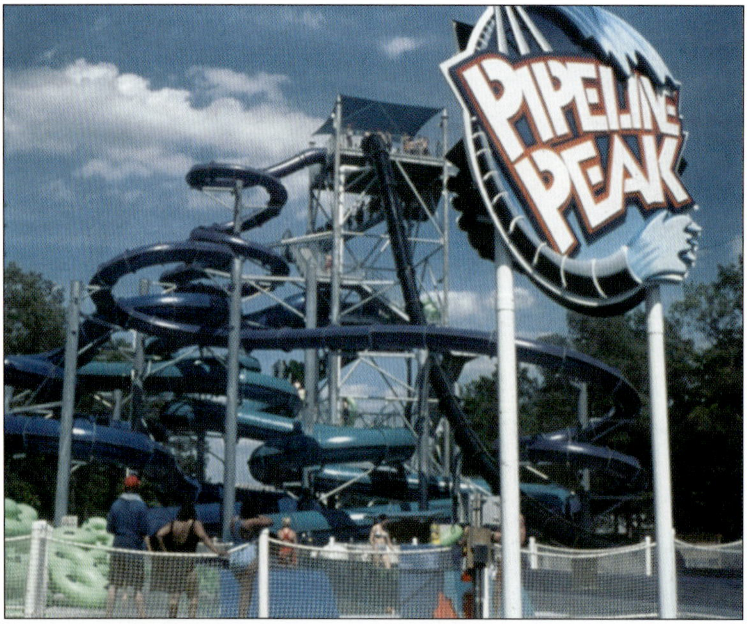

In 1999, Hurricane Reef water park was renamed WaterWorks in an expansion that included Big Wave Bay wave pool and Lil' Barefoot Beach for younger guests. The 2000 season saw the introduction of Pipeline Peak (pictured here). This massive new waterslide complex offered a variety of body and tube slides that all launched from a central tower.

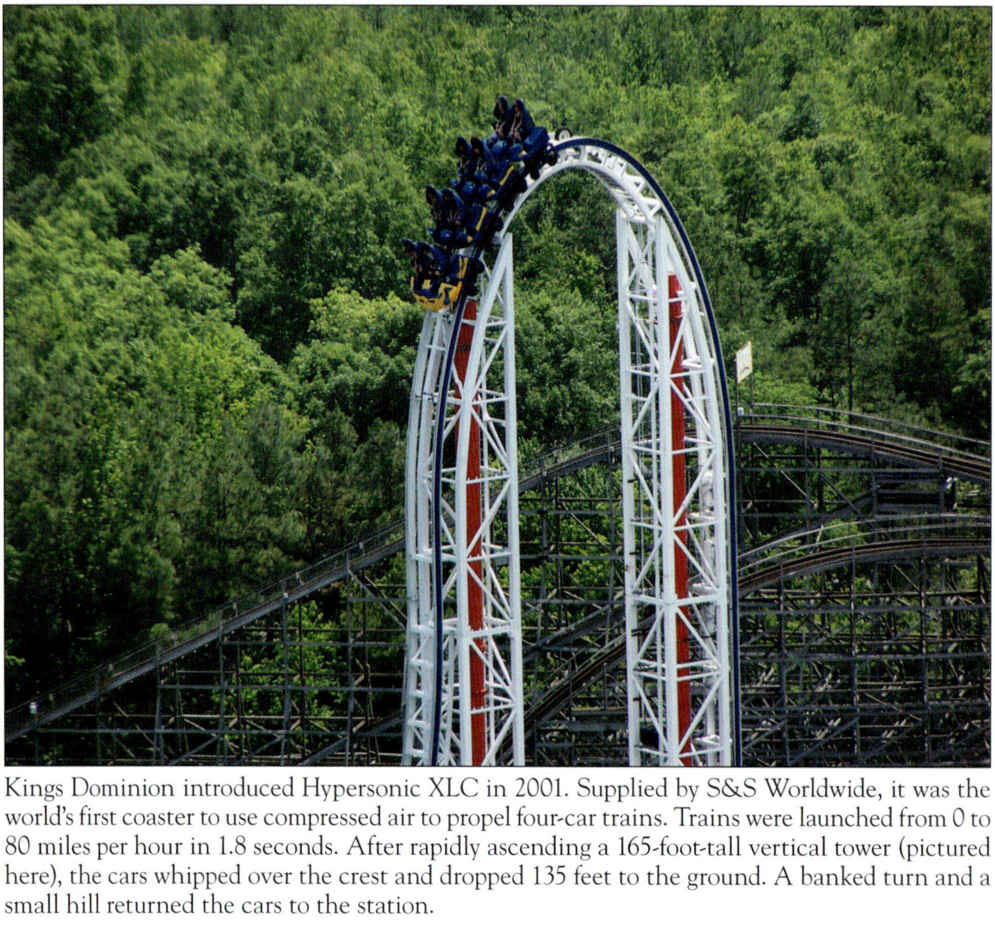

Kings Dominion introduced Hypersonic XLC in 2001. Supplied by S&S Worldwide, it was the world's first coaster to use compressed air to propel four-car trains. Trains were launched from 0 to 80 miles per hour in 1.8 seconds. After rapidly ascending a 165-foot-tall vertical tower (pictured here), the cars whipped over the crest and dropped 135 feet to the ground. A banked turn and a small hill returned the cars to the station.

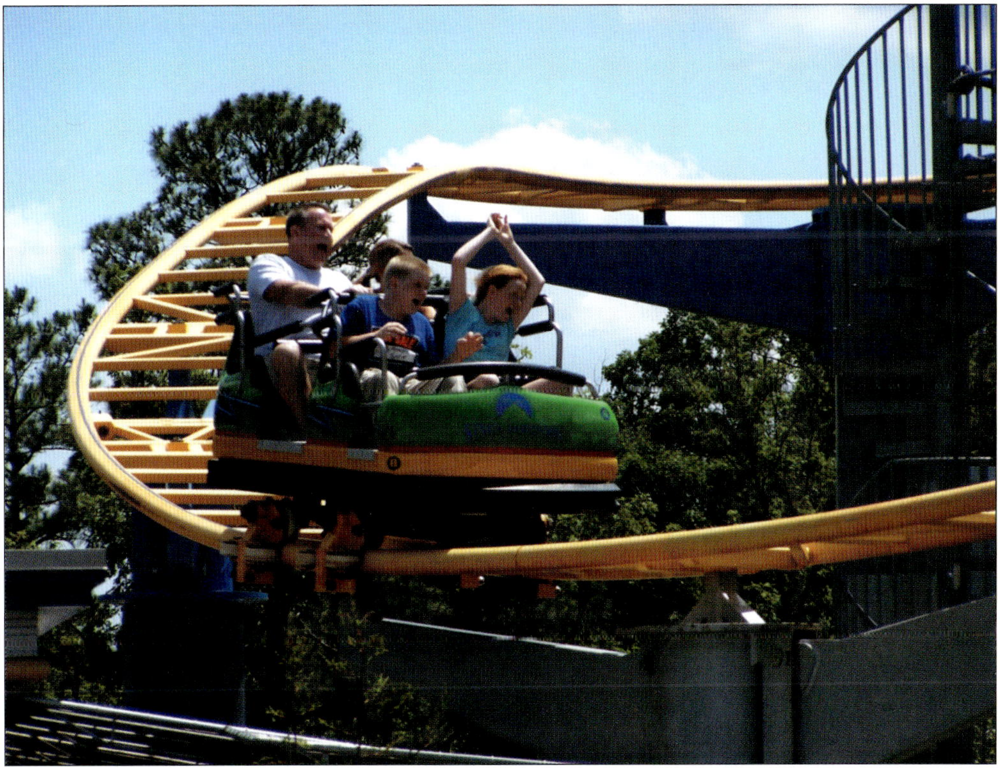

Though Kings Dominion's 2002 season saw the removal of Diamond Falls, it added two other attractions. The first was Ricochet, a compact steel Wild Mouse–style coaster. Manufactured by Germany's Mack Rides, Ricochet stood 52 feet tall and featured 1,312 feet of track. Ten individual four-seat cars thrilled riders on a track with several quick drops and tight hairpin turns.

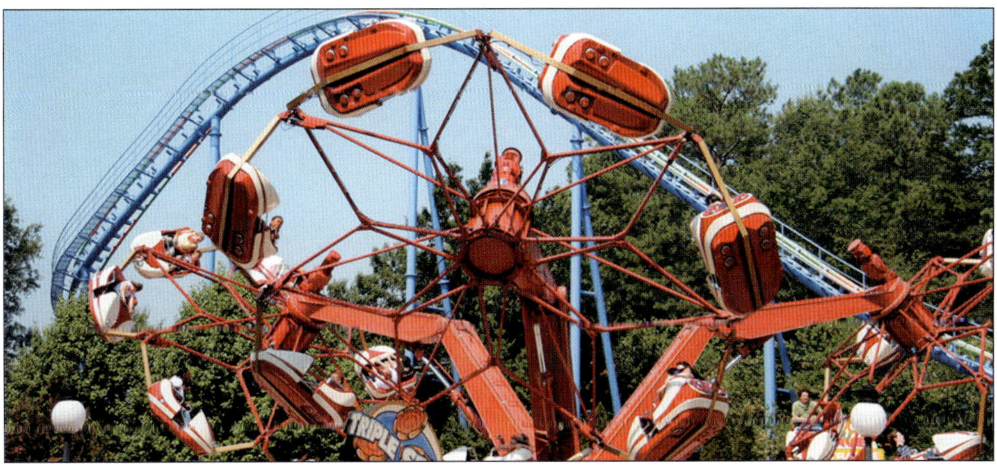

Triple Spin also joined the park's lineup in 2002. Taking up residence in front of Shockwave, Triple Spin was supplied by Germany's HUSS and goes by the trade name of Troika. Referring to the ride's three arms supporting the 21 two-seat rider pods, Troika is loosely translated from Russian to mean "grouping of three." In homage to the former Monster (page 30), the ride's name would be changed to Bad Apple in 2014 as part of the 40h Celebration.

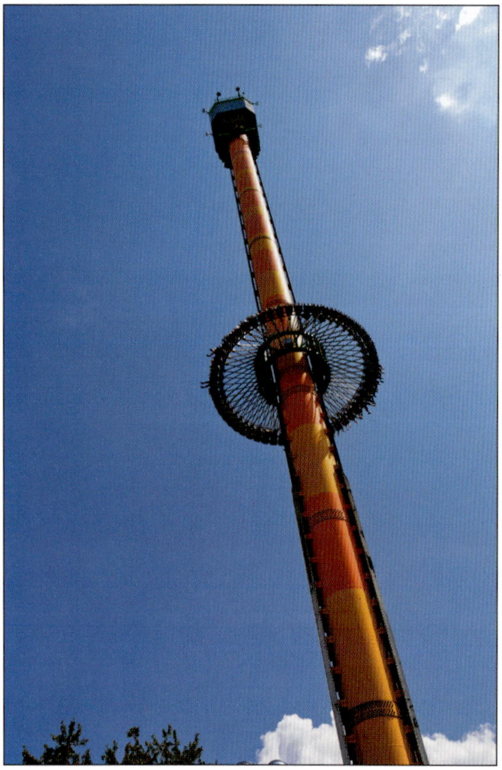

For the 2003 season, Kings Dominion opened Drop Zone: Stunt Tower. Another product of Intamin and known as a Gyro Tower, the ride took its name from the 1994 Paramount film *Drop Zone*. Standing 305 feet tall, the ride featured a gondola ringed with 56 seats. After being hauled to the top of the tower, the gondola was released into a 272-foot, 72-mile-per-hour free fall.

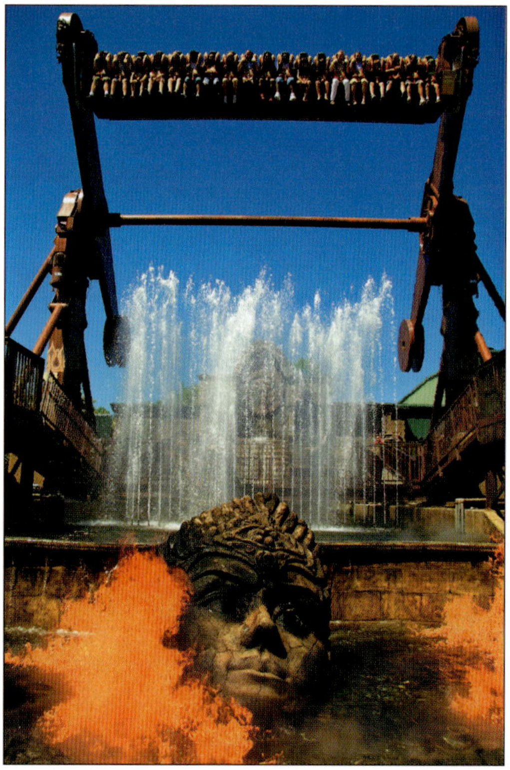

Tomb Raider: Firefall was added to the park for the 2005 season. Taking its thematic aspects from the Paramount films featuring Lara Croft: Tomb Raider, the attraction was a Top Spin produced by HUSS. Located near the Volcano, Tomb Raider: Firefall used fire, water, music, and other special effects as the large suspended gondola would subject riders to multiple rotations in both directions.

The Italian Job: Stunt Track would be the final Paramount-themed ride. Opened in 2006, the ride's theme borrowed from the film *The Italian Job*. Using LIMs for propulsion, the coaster featured three-car trains modeled after Mini Coopers. This was another collaboration between Werner Stengel and Premier Rides. The trains launched from the station (0–40 miles per hour in four seconds) and into a high-G upward spiral. (Courtesy Scott N. Rutherford.)

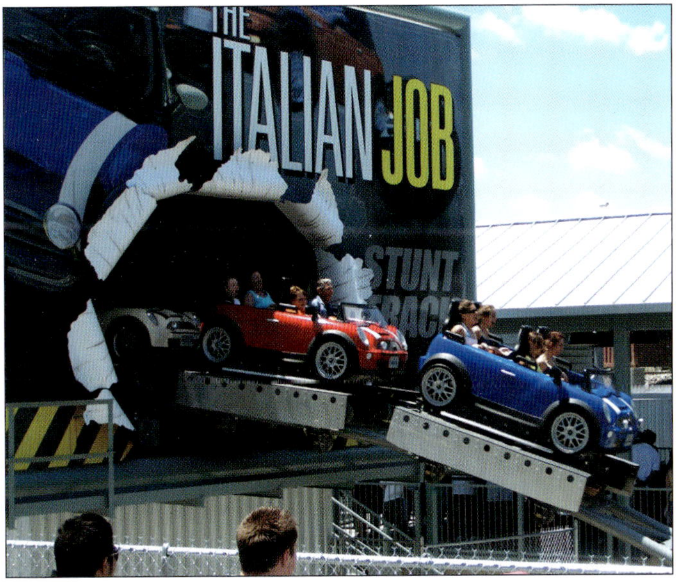

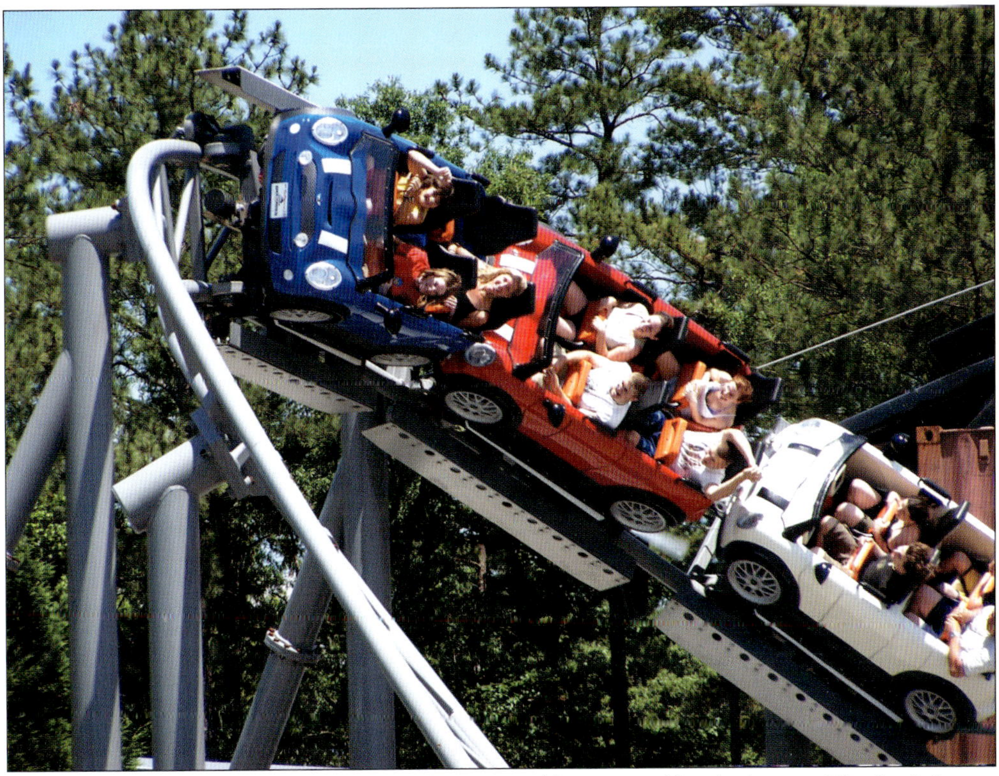

The 1,960-foot-long course offered quick drops, speed bumps, and banked turns. The finale began with the trains pausing for a moment (amid gunfire, a helicopter prop, and explosions) before being launched down into an enclosed "underground sewer" section that contained fast drops and banks in the dark. A third LIM boost propelled the trains out of the dark and through a billboard for a splashdown effect. (Courtesy Scott N. Rutherford.)

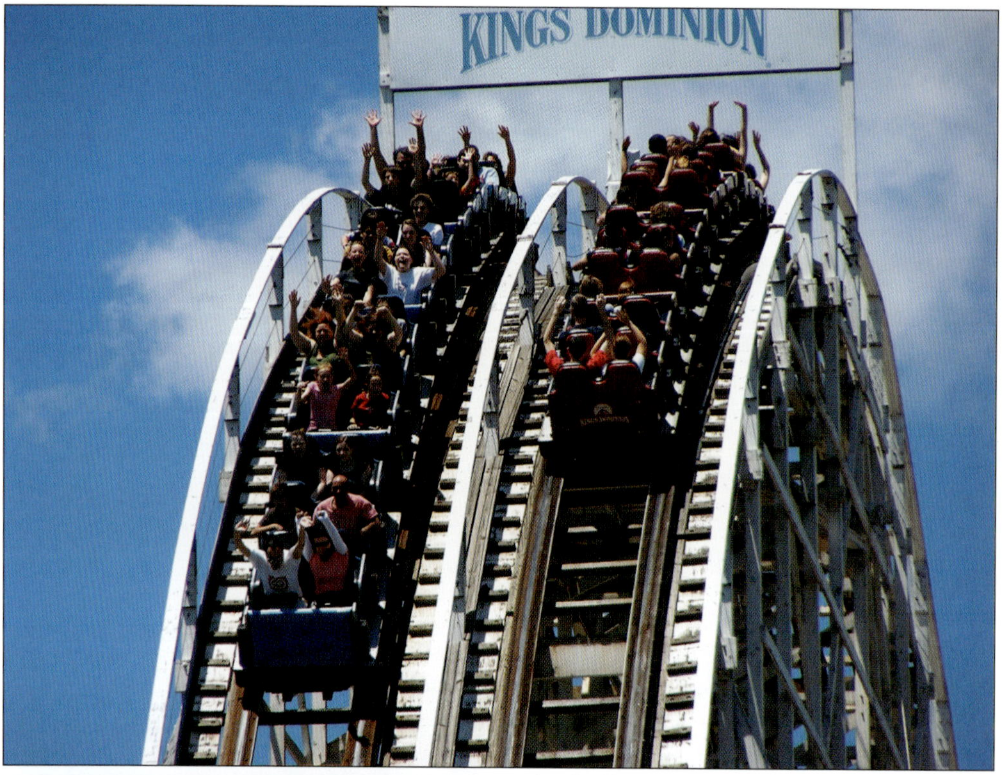

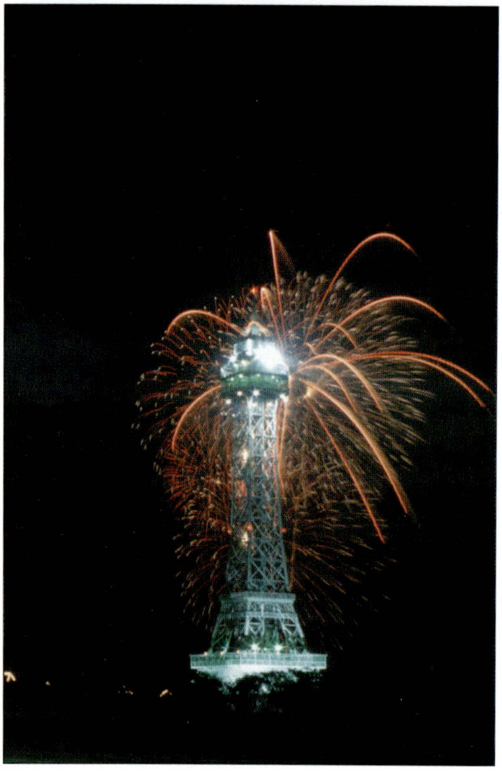

As the Paramount era drew to a close, guests got final rides on Backwards Rebel Yell. This image shows the red train facing the opposite direction. Reversing trains on wooden coasters was a trend started on The Racer at Kings Island (1982), Rebel Yell (1992,) and Thunder Road at Carowinds (1995). The trains would be soon turned back in the traditional direction. (Courtesy Scott N. Rutherford.)

Fireworks explode over the Eiffel Tower near the end of the 2006 season, which would be the final one under the Paramount stars. On June 30, Cedar Fair Entertainment Company purchased Paramount Parks from CBS Corporation for $1.25 billion. In many ways, Kings Dominion was a far different place than the one its original creators had first envisioned and opened three decades earlier.

Six

CEDAR FAIR

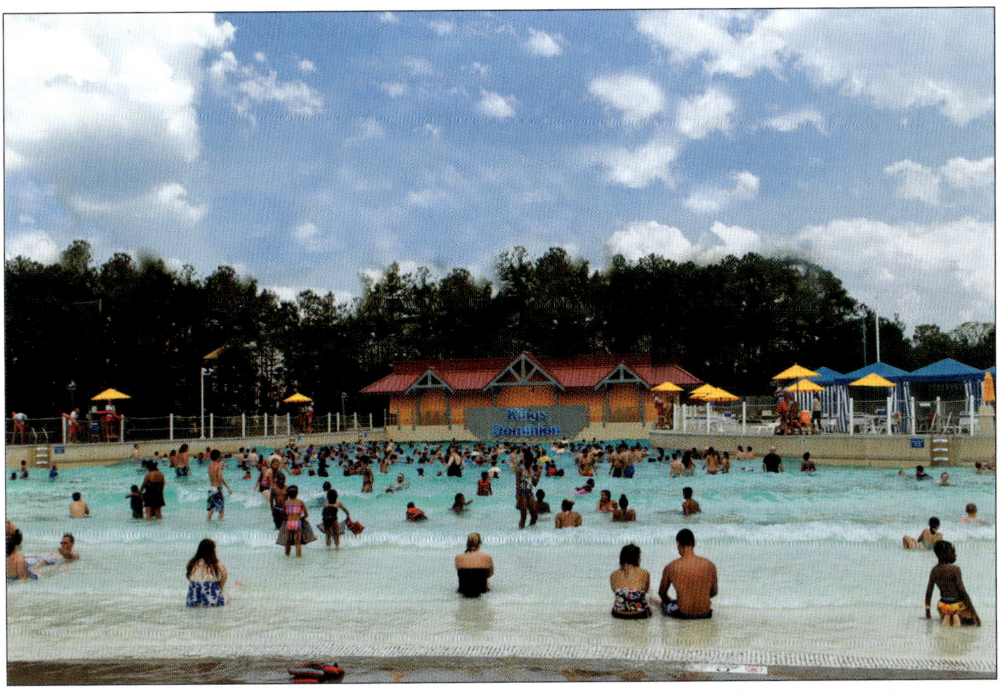

Many who had watched Kings Dominion evolve over the years, especially during the Paramount reign, saw this changing of the guard—with the Cedar Fair acquisition—as a good sign. Three new attractions were added in WaterWorks: Tidal Wave Bay (pictured here), Tornado, and Zoom Flume. An all-new Halloween event was introduced in the fall as FearFest was transformed into Halloween Haunt. This season would be the last for Hypersonic.

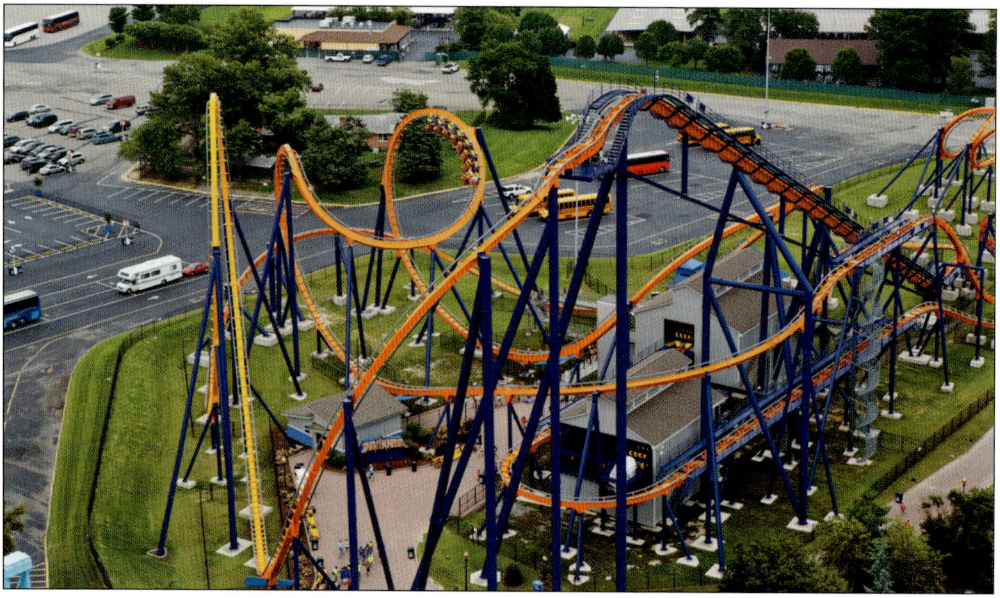

In 2008, Kings Dominion added to its lineup of world-class thrills by introducing Dominator, the park's 14th roller coaster. Supplied by renowned Swiss manufacturer Bolliger & Mabillard, the coaster was relocated from Ohio's shuttered Geauga Lake Park, where it operated from 2000 to 2007. (Courtesy Scott N. Rutherford.)

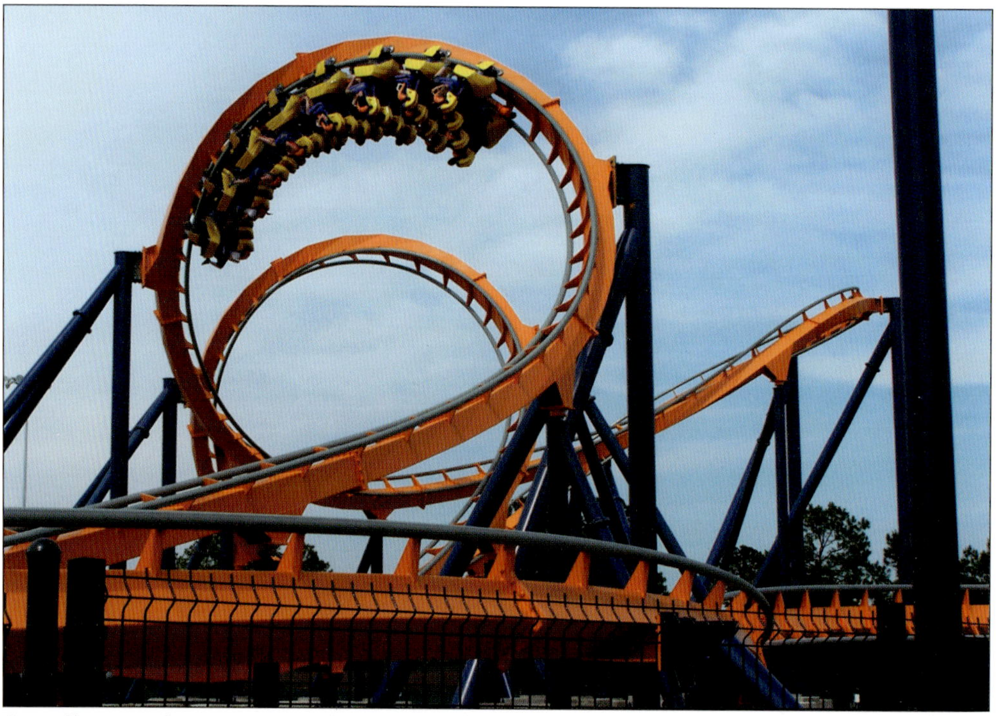

Actually erected in a repurposed section of the parking lot behind International Street near the Berserker, Dominator sent riders through five inversions at speeds up to 67 miles per hour on the world's longest floorless roller coaster (4,210 feet). The ride also boasts one of the largest vertical loops (135 feet) on the planet. (Courtesy Scott N. Rutherford.)

Kings Dominion's 2009 season was highlighted by two additional rides relocated from Geauga Lake: El Dorado (a HUSS swinging pendulum ride) and the Americana Ferris wheel. This shot captures Americana (and the renamed Drop Tower: Scream Zone) in the soft, rich light of the setting summer sun. (Courtesy Scott N. Rutherford.)

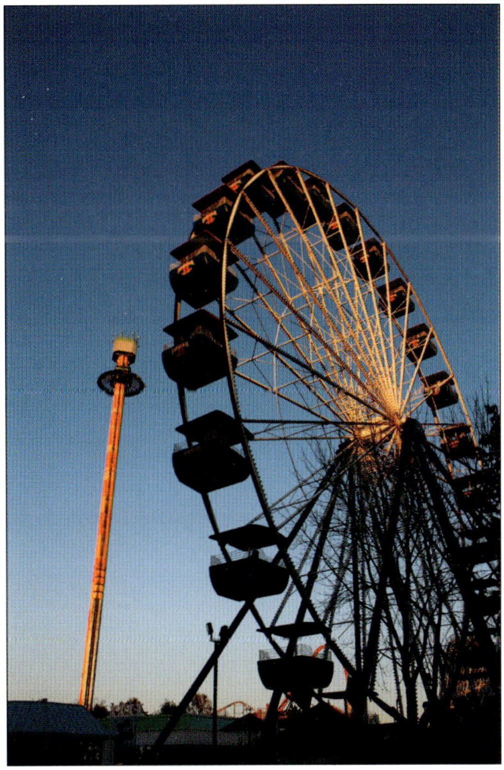

The Grizzly also received some love in 2009 in the form of a major part of the layout being re-tracked. This action provided guests with a smoother, more enjoyable ride experience aboard one of the park's most popular rides. Pictured here is Grizzly's yellow train headed toward the final turn. The enclosed structure below the train is the coaster's infamous tunnel, which contains a hidden speed bump. (Courtesy Scott N. Rutherford.)

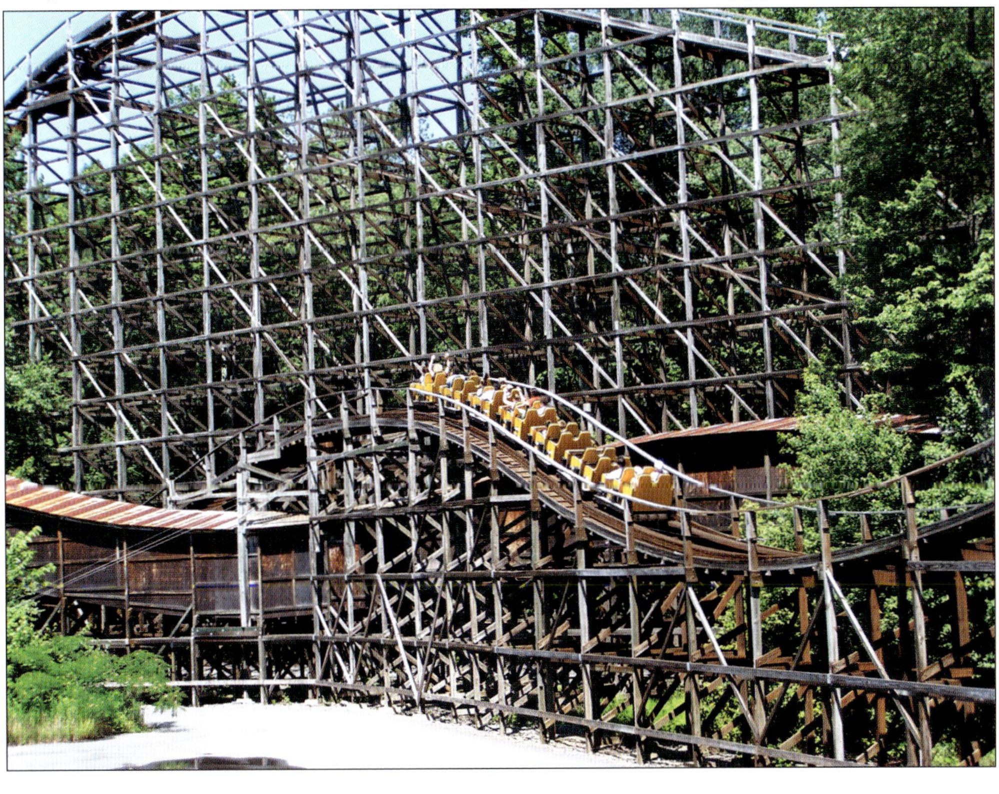

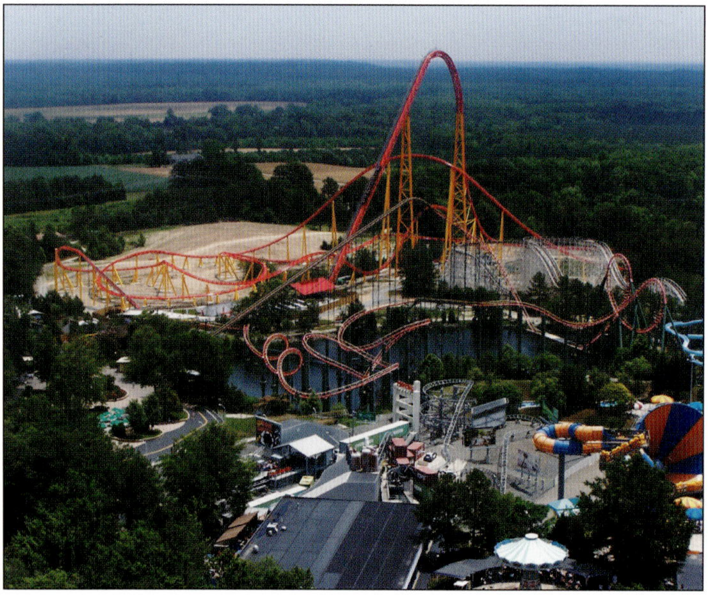

In 2010, Kings Dominion unveiled Intimidator 305 (also known as I-305), an Intamin Giga Coaster. The $25 million investment was the largest of any ride in the park's history. It was named and themed after the late NASCAR driver Dale Earnhardt (also known as "the Intimidator"). The ride was voted "Best New Roller Coaster of 2010" in *Amusement Today* magazine's coveted Golden Ticket Awards. (Courtesy Scott N. Rutherford.)

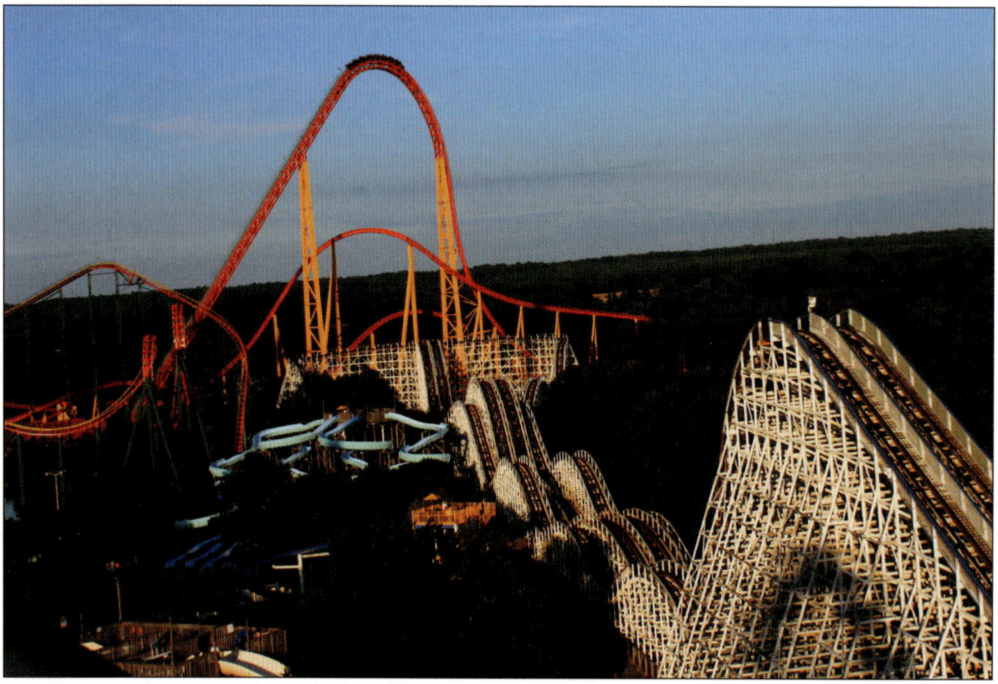

Standing 305 feet tall, the ride was built on land previously occupied by parts of Lion Country Safari. In this late afternoon shot taken from the Americana Ferris wheel, the train is poised on the precipice. Soon, riders will race down the 300-foot first drop and achieve speeds over 90 miles per hour. Both Rebel Yell on the right and Anaconda on the left seem miniature in the shadow of I-305. (Courtesy Scott N. Rutherford.)

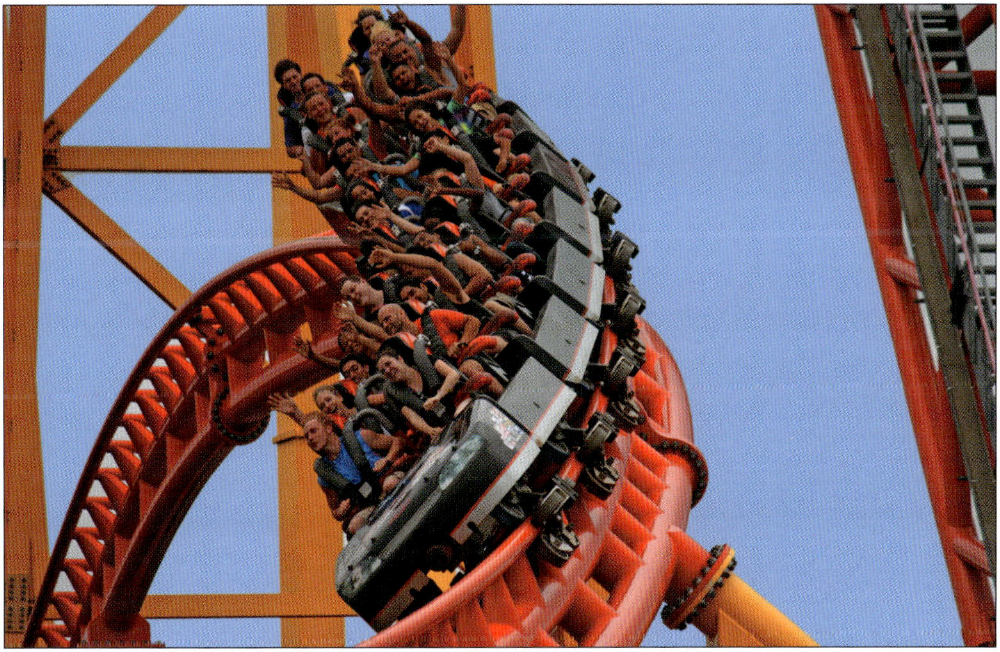

Following its 30-story, 85-degree first drop, the remainder of I-305's 5,100-foot-long course was peppered with abrupt changes in direction that challenged every rider's equilibrium. This view illustrates just one the coaster's many extreme twists and turns, which are taken at full speed. Despite I-305's radical nature, riders are kept safely in their seats with a beefy but comfortable lap bar and upper body restraints. (Courtesy Scott N. Rutherford.)

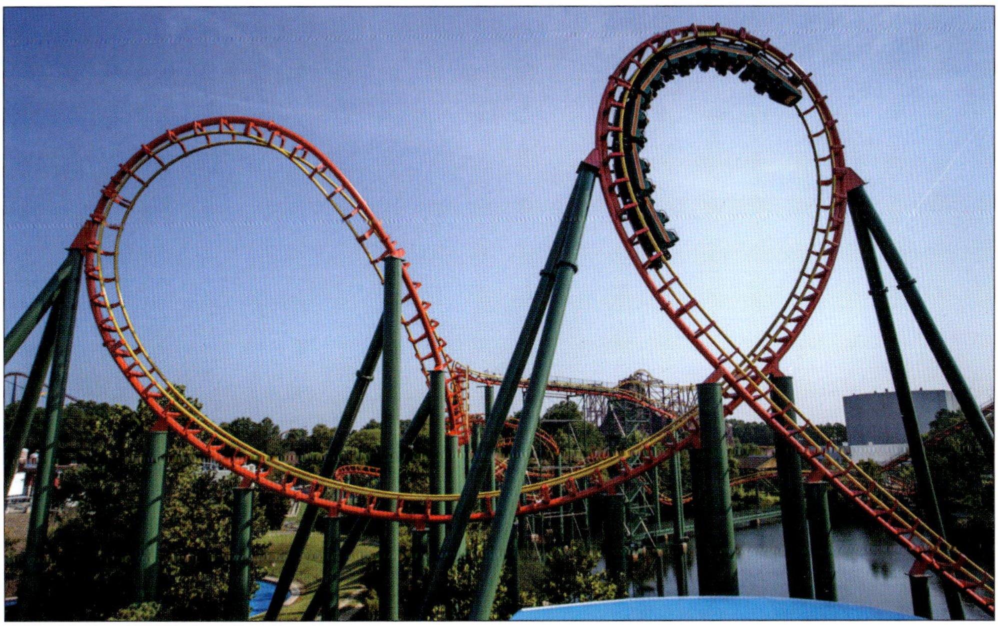

Complimenting I-305's bold color scheme, Anaconda received some new paint of its own. Here, in this shot captured from the water park, the train is racing up into its vertical loop, which will lead smoothly through the sidewinder. The Volcano and Flight of Fear coasters are in the background.

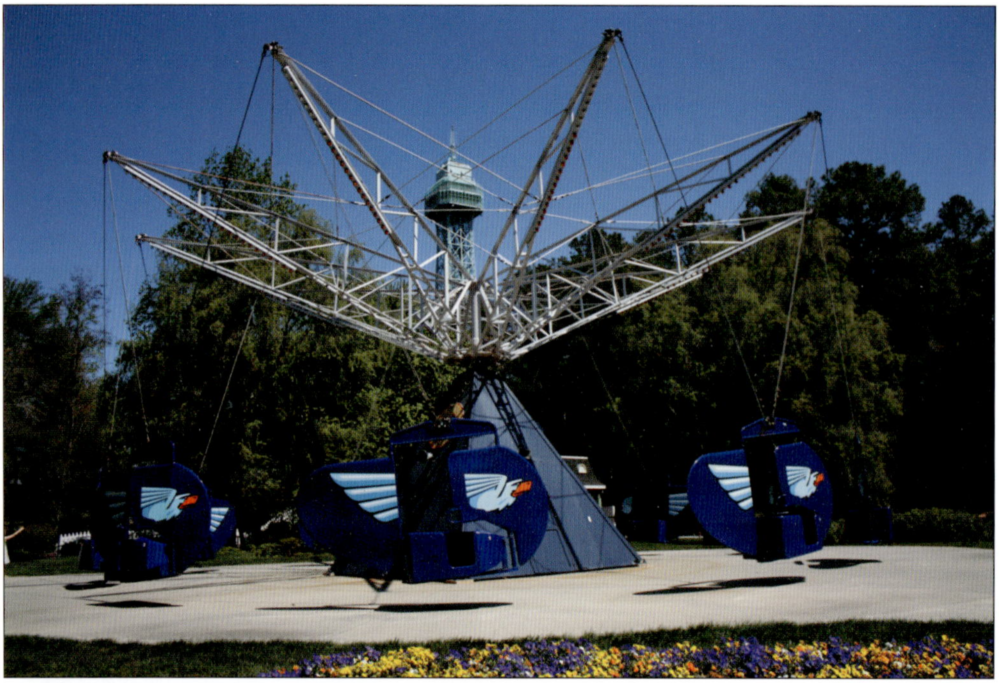

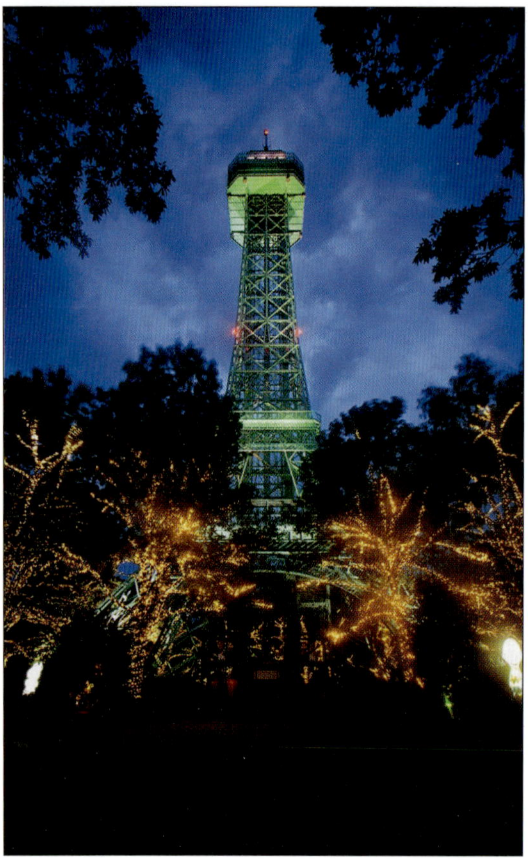

While so many of Kings Dominion's original rides were lost for one reason or another, the park's Flying Scooter has endured. Pictured here in its current home in Old Virginia, this timeless classic is now known as the Flying Eagles. Like it has for the past 70-plus years, it remains a guest favorite. (Courtesy Scott N. Rutherford.)

Snoopy's Starlight Spectacular premiered in 2011. This after-dark event featuring Snoopy and the Peanuts characters used a mix of low energy/high efficiency LED illumination that immersed guests in a walk-through world of light and music. The center walkway leading from the Eiffel Tower to the Grove and midway area featured characters, animated light displays, and a choreographed audio soundtrack. (Courtesy Scott N. Rutherford.)

Kings Dominion continued its theme of giant rides in 2012 with the introduction of WindSeeker. This towering swing ride, supplied by Mondial of the Netherlands, was a sight to behold. Located in the Grove, WindSeeker featured 32 suspended open-air seats that took 64 riders in pairs 300 feet into the air, spinning them around at 30 miles per hour. An onboard audio system as well as an LED lighting package enhances guest experience.

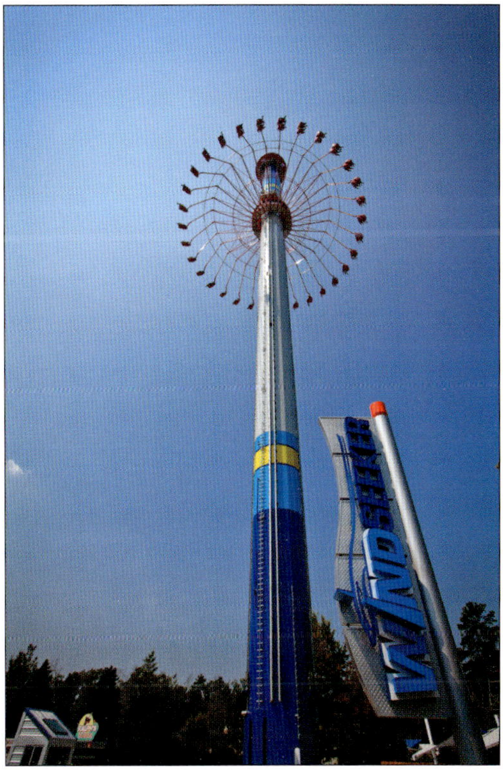

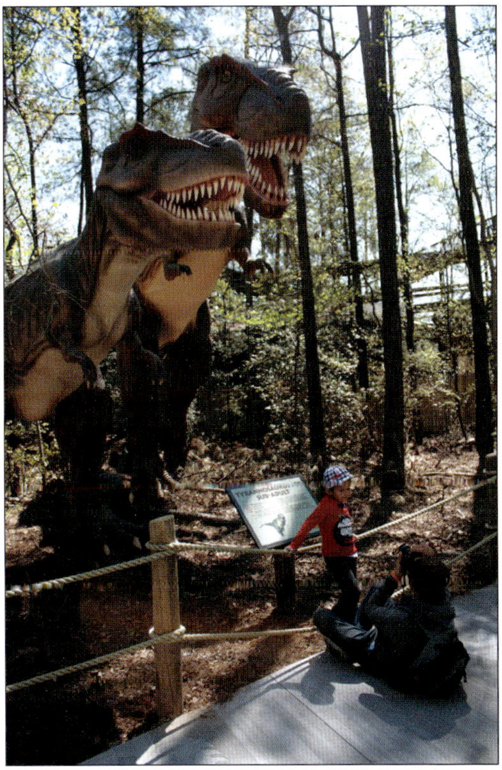

Also new for 2012 was Dinosaurs Alive!, an outdoor walk-through attraction that combined life-size animatronics, interactive consoles, and educational content about how the dinosaurs lived and behaved. Located in a dense forest behind Grizzly, the self-guided tour requires an additional charge. As a companion experience, *Dinosaurs: Monsters of Patagonia*, a 3-D film narrated by Donald Sutherland, is presented in the Action Theater. (Courtesy Scott N. Rutherford.)

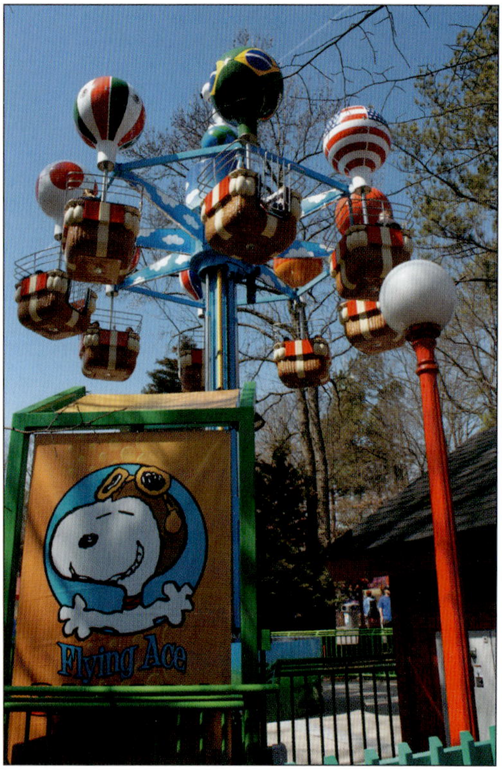

For the 2013 season, Planet Snoopy was expanded to incorporate the KidZville area. Known now as the Bigger, Better Planet Snoopy, Kings Dominion could now boast to being home to the world's largest Peanuts-themed area. The new Planet Snoopy also contained a number of new rides supplied by Italian manufacturer Zamperla. Pictured here is the Flying Ace Balloon Race. (Courtesy Scott N. Rutherford.)

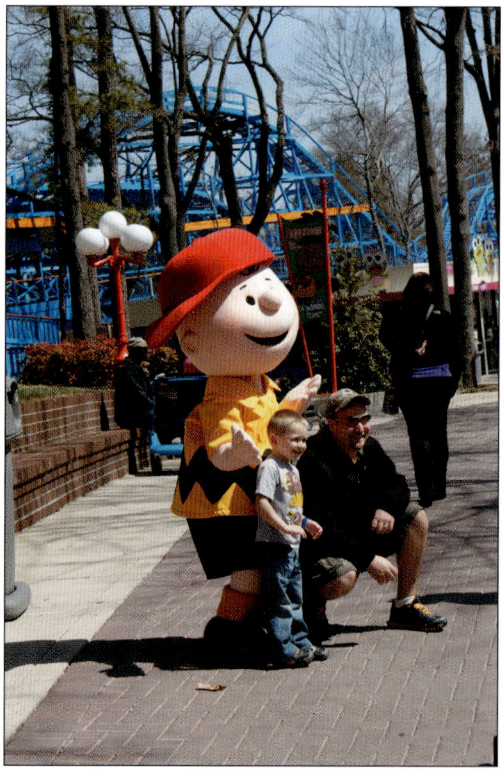

Kings Dominion's Bigger, Better Planet Snoopy continued the time-honored tradition of character encounters. Here, a father and son pose for a photograph with Charlie Brown. Just as when the park first opened, meeting a live character from one's favorite cartoon or comic leaves a lasting impression. (Courtesy Scott N. Rutherford.)

Kings Dominion's 2014 season will be remembered as extra special due to the launching of the park's 40th Celebration, marking four decades of fun at the Virginia themer. Since facets of the park opened both in 1974 and 1975, the 40th Celebration would encompass 2014 and 2015. Banners like this one went up around the park while a number of other changes made these two seasons memorable. (Courtesy Scott N. Rutherford.)

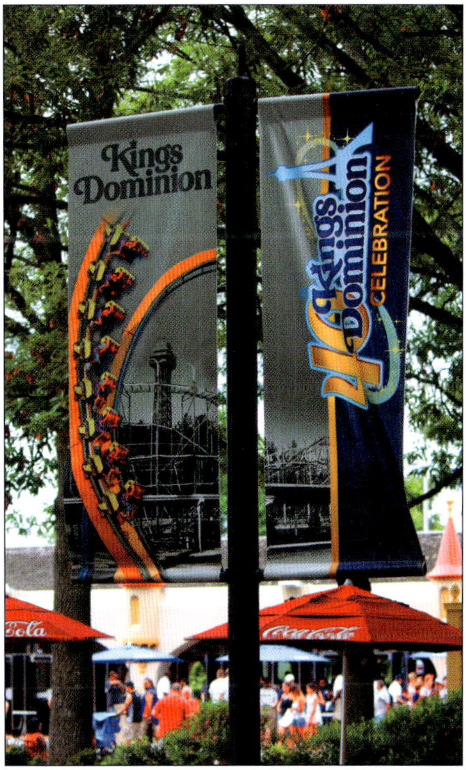

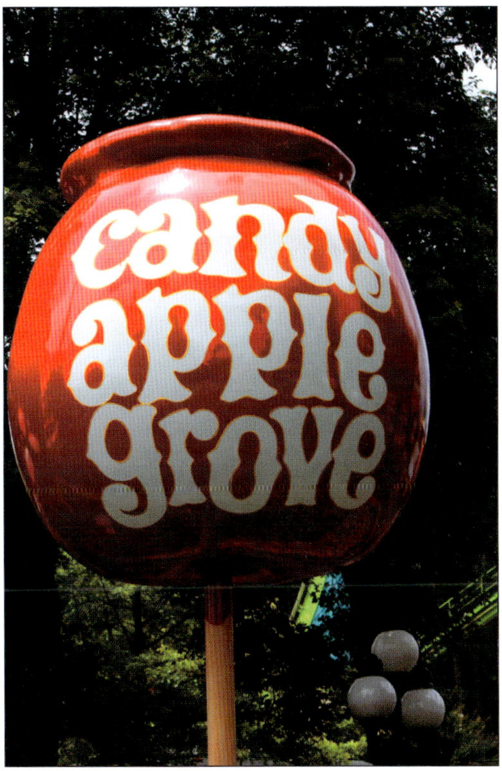

One of the most significant aspects of the 40th Celebration was the rebranding of the Grove back into Candy Apple Grove. For many, that name evokes the sweetest of memories. Along with many new features, Cedar Fair brought back plenty of other beloved aspects of this section, such as the large red candy apples on sticks, and they renamed Triple Spin as the Bad Apple (the former Monster ride was once known as Bad Apple).

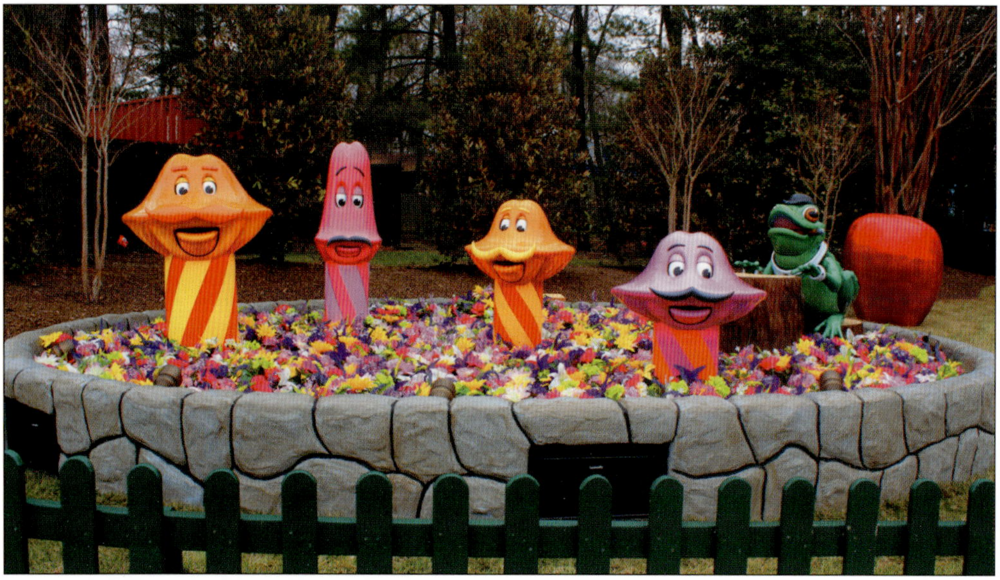

Another highlight of the park's 40th Celebration was the return of the iconic Singing Mushrooms. This fan-favorite featured four colorful mushrooms along with a piano-playing frog all singing favorite barbershop quartet tunes.

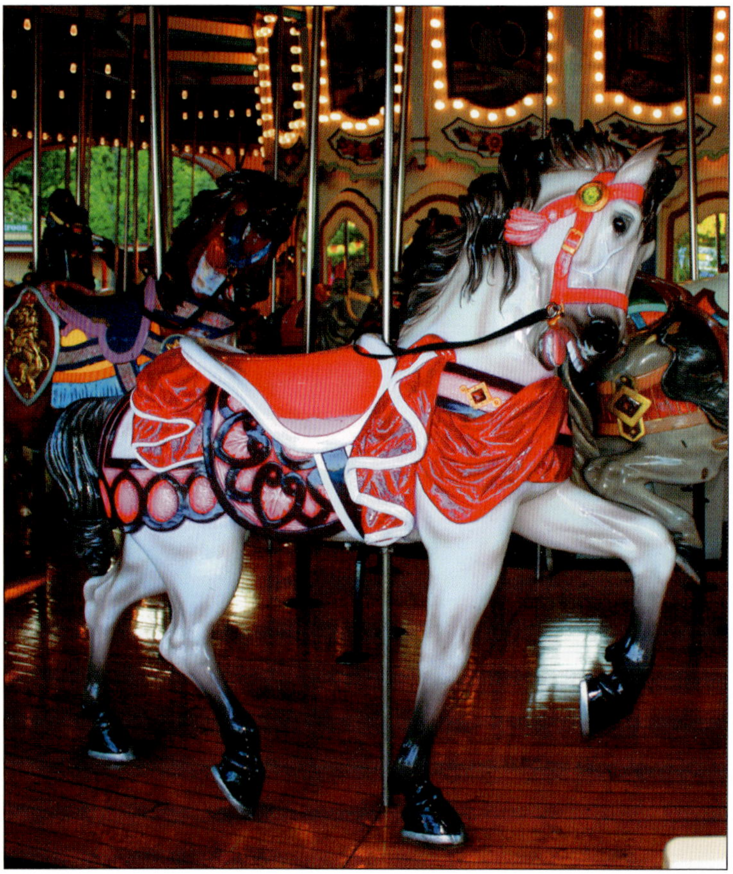

The centerpiece of the 40th Celebration was the introduction of Ruby, a custom-painted horse added to the park's historic carousel. The addition of Ruby capped off an ambitious multiphase overhaul and rehabilitation of the carousel that was finished just in time for the park's milestone 40th the season. The park also changed Congo back to Safari Village. (Courtesy Scott N. Rutherford.)

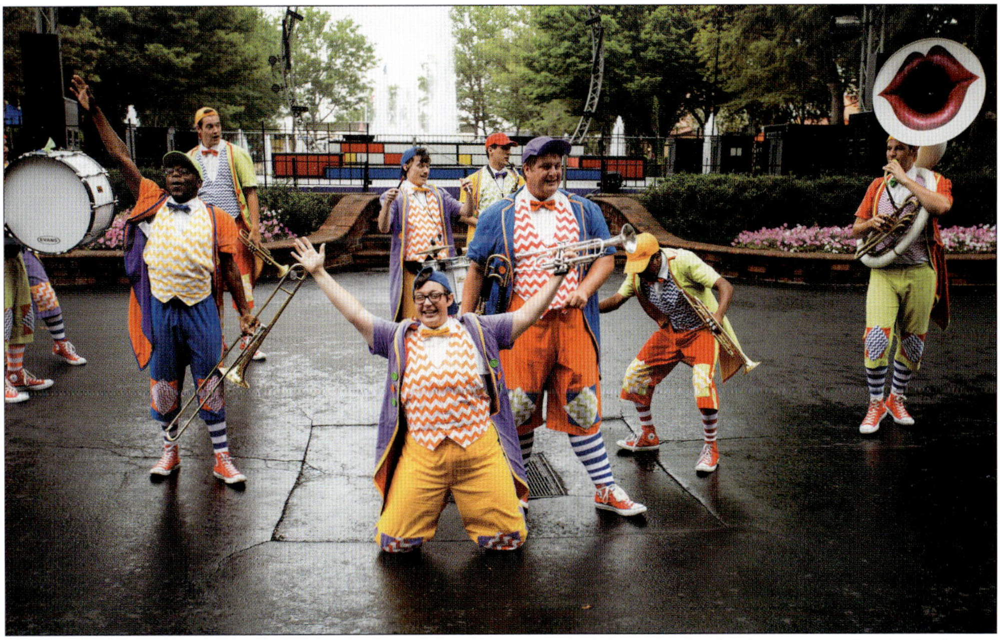

Another aspect of the 40th Celebration was the return of the comical Clown Band. The beloved performing group from Kings Dominion's past was back with plenty of surprises. Roving along the midways, the Clown Band interacts with guests while entertaining with a selection of popular songs and outlandish antics. (Courtesy Scott N. Rutherford.)

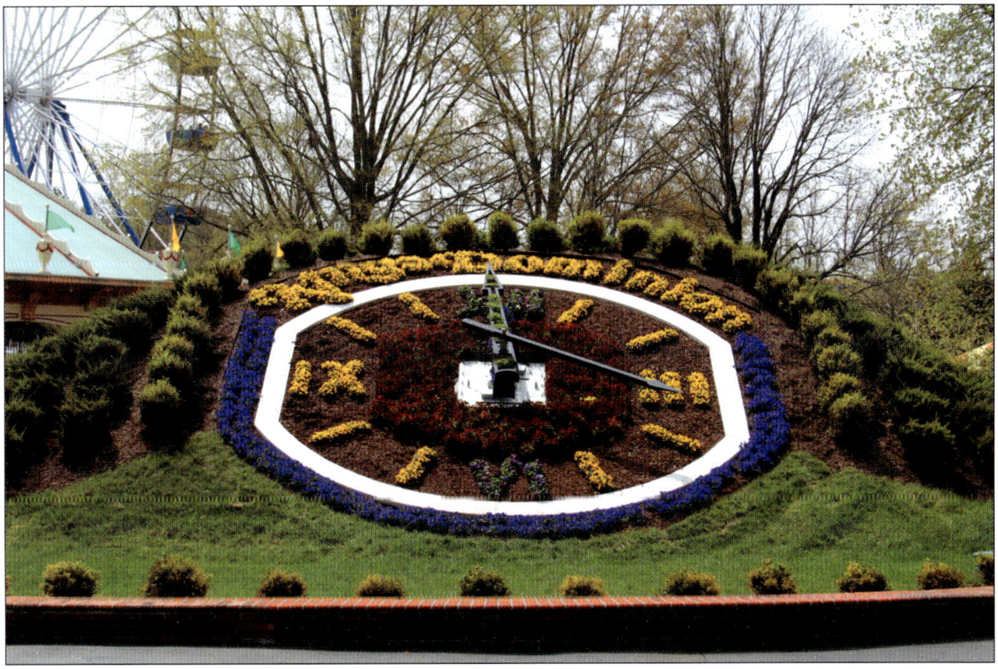

While virtually the entire park got a fresh coat of paint and other accoutrements in honor of the 40th Celebration, the popular Floral Clock was also completely rebuilt for the occasion. While simple in execution, this functioning timepiece offers an esthetic beauty that is missing in many of today's modern parks.

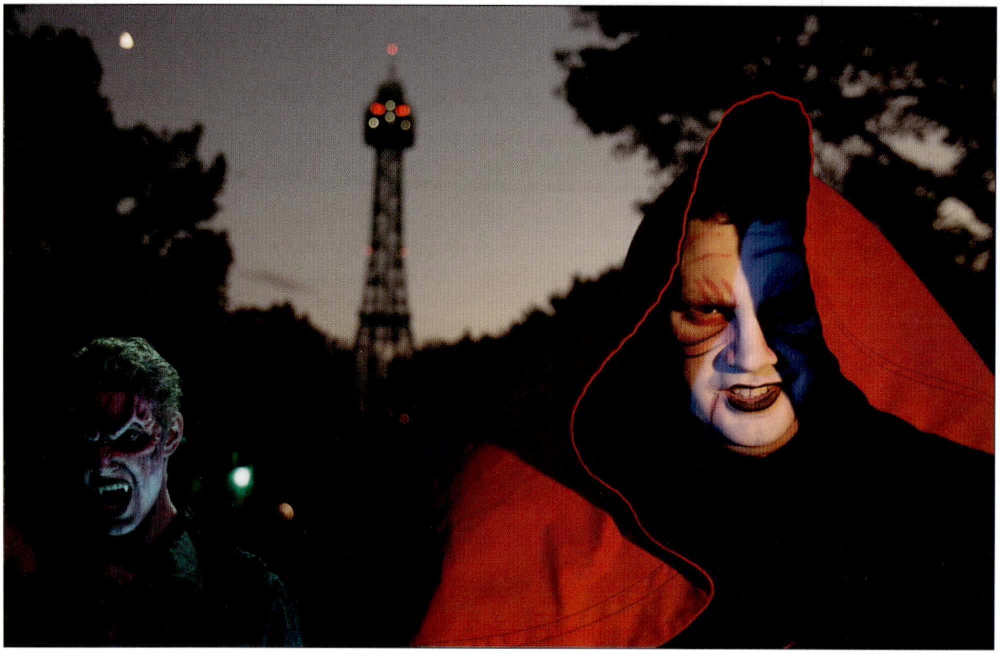

Held each autumn, Kings Dominion's Halloween Haunt is an annual nighttime event that features a large number of mazes, scare zones, and actors dressed up as terrifying creatures. These include ghosts, vampires, werewolves, and serial killers. In addition, the majority of the park's roller coasters and other thrill rides operate during the popular Halloween Haunt.

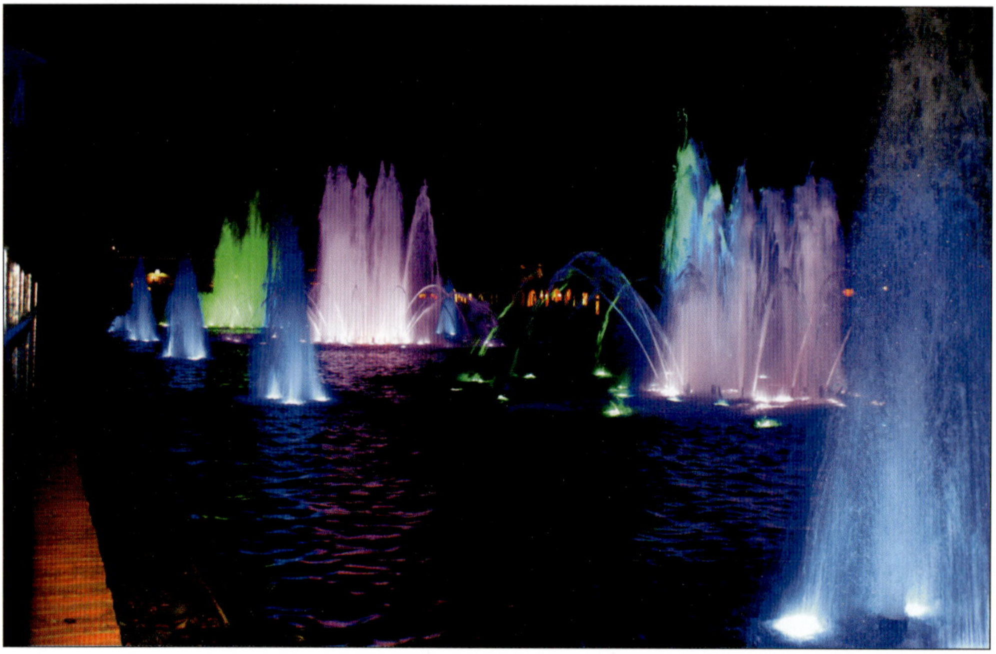

The Royal Fountain on International Street received a complete overhaul for the 40th Celebration. An all-new computerized lighting system works to bring the water to life in an ever-changing presentation of color and motion. The fountains and the iconic Eiffel Tower make this area one of the park's most popular photograph spots. (Courtesy Scott N. Rutherford.)

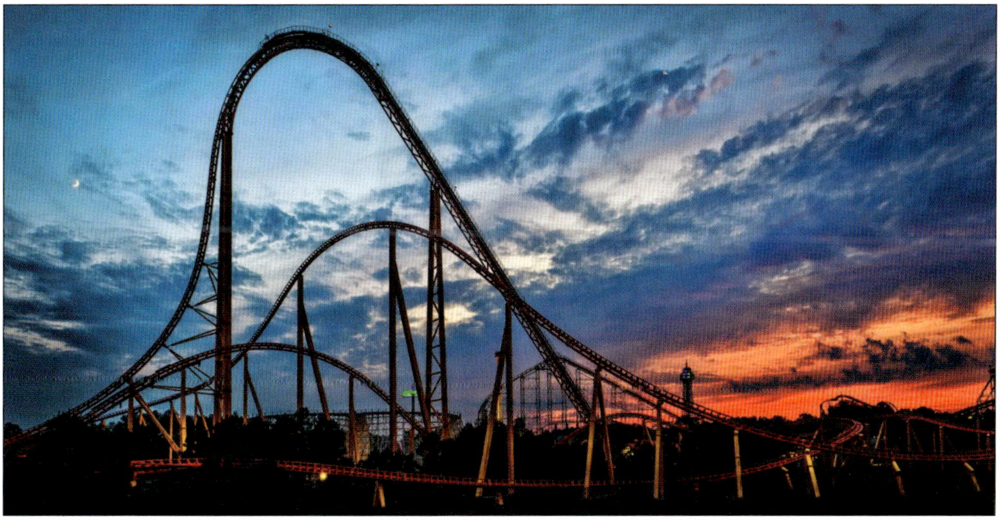

The people who built and worked at Kings Dominion helped transform it into a place for families and friends to come together and make lasting memories. It is a safe bet that the summers ahead will offer guests the same combination of southern hospitality and one-of-a-kind thrills. Happy 40th birthday, Kings Dominion!

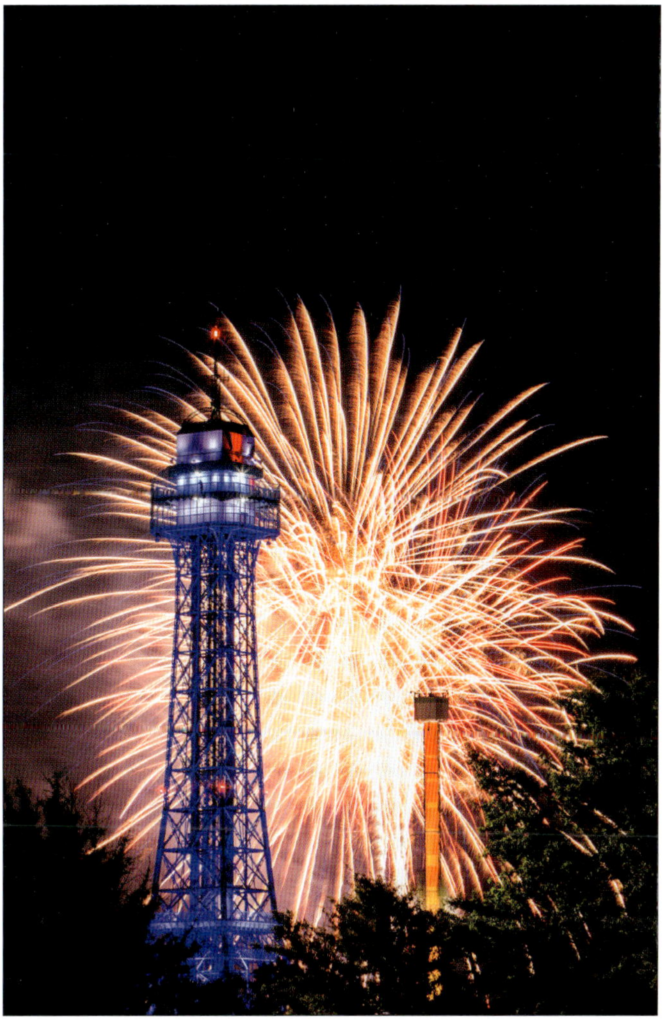